MARCO ⊕ POLO

COSTA BRAVA

BARCELONA

with Local Tips
*The author's special recommendations are
highlighted in yellow throughout this guide*

There are five symbols to help you find your way around this guide:

★

Marco Polo's top recommendations – the best in each category

sites wi...

places where...

D0682256

⊼

places where young people get together

(100/A1)
pages and coordinates for the Road Atlas of the Costa Brava
(U/A1) *coordinates for the City Map of Barcelona inside back cover*
(O) *areas not covered by the City Map*
*For your orientation even places that are not marked in the Road Atlas
are provided with coordinates.*

*This guide was written by Norbert Lewandowski,
who is an author of numerous travel guides. He reports
regularly from Spain, especially from Catalonia.*

MARCO ⊕ POLO

Travel guides and language guides in this series:

Alaska • Algarve • Amsterdam • Australia/Sydney • Bahamas • Barbados
Barcelona • Berlin • Brittany • Brussels • California • Canada • Channel Islands
Chicago and the Great Lakes • Copenhagen • Costa Brava/Barcelona
Costa del Sol/Granada • Crete • Cuba • Cyprus • Dominican Republic
Eastern Canada • Eastern USA • Egypt • Florence • Florida • French Riviera
Gran Canaria • Greek Islands/Aegean • Hong Kong • Ibiza/Formentera
Ireland • Israel • Istanbul • Italian Riviera • Jamaica • Lanzarote • London
Los Angeles • Madeira • Mallorca • Malta • Menorca •Mexico • Netherlands
New York • New Zealand • Normandy • Norway • Paris • Portugal • Prague
Rhodes • Rocky Mountains • Rome • San Francisco • Scotland • South
Africa • Southwestern USA • Switzerland • Tenerife • Thailand • Turkish
Coast • Tuscany • USA: New England • USA: Southern States • Venice
Washington D.C. •Western Canada • Western USA

French • German • Italian • Spanish

*Marco Polo would be very interested to hear your
comments and suggestions. Please write to:*

North America:
Marco Polo North America
70 Bloor Street East
Oshawa, Ontario, Canada
(B) 905-436-2525

United Kingdom:
GeoCenter International Ltd
The Viables Centre
Harrow Way
Basingstoke, Hants RG22 4BJ

*Our authors have done their research very carefully, but should any errors or omissions
have occurred, the publisher cannot be held responsible for any injury, damage
or inconvenience suffered due to incorrect information in this guide*

Cover photograph: Lloret de Mar (Schuster/Prisma)
Photos: G. Amberg (34); author (46, 66); O. Baumli (12, 29, 68, 79, 80); R. Gill (14);
K. Kallabis (52); Lade: Höber (40), Pictures (64); Mauritius: Hubatka (99);
Schapowalow: Schäfer (60); A. Sperber (18); O. Stadler (20, 23, 74, 81, 87);
M. Thomas (4, 6, 10, 15, 24, 26, 43, 50, 55, 70); Transglobe: Bauer (96)

2nd revised edition 2001
© Mairs Geographischer Verlag, Ostfildern, Germany
Translator: Jane Riester
English edition 2001: Gaia Text, Munich
Editorial director: Ferdinand Ranft
Chief editor: Marion Zorn
Cartography for the Road Atlas: © Mairs Geographischer Verlag
Design and layout: Thienhaus/Wippermann
Printed in Germany

CONTENTS

Introduction: Discover the Costa Brava! 5
*Images of the Costa Brava: fishing villages and beaches,
tourist centres, sleepy medieval hamlets – and everywhere
you look, Salvador Dalí has left his Surrealist mark*

History at a glance 11

Costa Brava in context: Moors, artists and Sardana 13
*Catalonia has a culture all its own:
a cursory look at the Costa Brava*

Food & drink: Culinary pot-pourri of unusual recipes 21
*Costa Brava cuisine: a captivating combination
of seemingly incompatible ingredients*

Shopping & souvenirs: Leather, fashion, junk 25
*A shopping spree in the shops, boutiques and markets
offers something for every pocket*

Events: Fiestas and festivals 27
Dances and processions abound all year round

Short tour of Barcelona 30

Hotel and restaurant prices 35

North Coast: Fishing villages and artists' colonies 35
Sit back and relax in picturesque bays and cosy bars

Gulf of Roses: Historical landscape by the sea 47
*Both Greeks and Romans left their mark on the
Riu Fluvià delta*

Central Costa Brava: The heart of the Costa Brava 61
Medieval towns, cork oak groves and first-rate fish cuisine

South Coast: Tourism for the masses on the wild coast 75
*Water sports and endless nights for international guests –
young people drawn to the discos and the beach*

Routes on the Costa Brava 89

Essentials: Practical information 93
*Important addresses and useful information for
your visit to the Costa Brava*

Do's and don'ts 98

Road Atlas of the Costa Brava 99

Index 115

What do you get for your money? 116

Discover the Costa Brava!

Images of the Costa Brava: fishing villages and beaches, tourist centres, sleepy medieval hamlets – and everywhere you look, Salvador Dalí has left his Surrealist mark

The true nature of the Costa Brava is best revealed to the traveller who scales one of the fairly steep mountain paths. Picture the scene: the September sun is at its peak, beating down on you mercilessly; the contours of your destination – the ruins of a thousand-year-old monastery – seem to swim in the heat-hazy air, its grey-brown walls baked to the same colour as the surrounding barren landscape. The only sound is made by the crickets, whirring like countless electric motors. You're perspiring heavily, your throat is parched – why torture yourself like this for a few old stones? Sights like these are to be found all over the place, surely? Instinctively you glance back over your shoulder: how far have I got? The view seems unending; no man-made or natural barriers interrupt the panorama. Neither the semicircular bay, marked by its sparkling white fishing village straight out of a holiday brochure, nor the jagged crown of the cliffs

Bizarre cliffs and sandy coves: typical of the Costa Brava

jutting out of the sea, or the mountains, which, like a curtain, conceal the next picture-postcard image. In the distance, where the blue of the sky dissolves into the azure sea, where the eye struggles to discern boundaries, surely that is where the "other" Costa Brava lies, the tourist magnet? But here, for the moment, this is the only Costa Brava – too beautiful to be true? You're hooked!

Change of scene: it's late in the evening and you are sitting at a street café in Cadaqués, enjoying a moment of peace after your meal. Sit back and relax, no sudden movements, no loud noises, thank you. Suddenly the silence is broken by the rattling engine of a moped circling the Plaça. No silencer, of course, and the sound sets your delicate Anglo-Saxon nerves on edge, to put it mildly. You're too lazy, though, to get up. Round and round he goes. You feel a cold dog's nose in your hand, one of those strays you see on the beach. Strange, but you suddenly become aware of the starry sky, lit up like a fairground, and the façades of the houses along the sea front, bathed in pale moonlight.

You notice the gentle lapping of the waves, drowning out even the sound of the moped – who cares? You're hooked again – on the Costa Brava?

But wait – you visitors ought to take a look at Lloret or Platja d'Aro. Costa Brava? Costa del Concrete more like it! Such is the opinion of many with a more critical eye – and they're not all wrong, it must be said. Further south, there are no more ruined monasteries and it's not only the dog's noses that are cold, but also the souls of the cool and calculating tourism managers. There are more mopeds, too – approximately 50,000 in fact. There just aren't enough stars in the sky to contend with that!

Images of a landscape. Costa Brava the beautiful? Or the ugly? Which description fits? If we look at things from a purely scientific point of view, we have to admit that man has only rarely managed to enhance a landscape;

Disneyland, for example, or the icing-on-the-cake ornamental gardens of feudal princes. Joking aside, though, hasn't the Costa Brava always been beautiful?

For some 2,600 or 2,700 years, the west coast of the Mediterranean has attracted foreigners as if by magic. From the other end of the Mediterranean came the Phoenicians from Asia Minor, then the Greeks from the Aegean. They were succeeded by the Carthaginians from North Africa who sought to establish a bridgehead against the Romans on this stretch of coast. They had not bargained on the Romans themselves taking an interest in the area in their own right and were promptly sent packing! The new world power from Rome had a foothold here for quite some time, about 600 years in fact. Finally, the restless Visigoths marched in from the north, leaving their cold homelands behind. Another 300 years later, Arabs ar-

Coastline near Tossa de Mar at the southern end of the Costa Brava

rived from North Africa (maybe they were fleeing from the heat!). This tempted Charlemagne and his Franks into the arena, leading incidentally to an episode that gave Catalonia its national colours: four red stripes on a yellow background. Wilfred the Bearded (in Catalan, Guifre el Pilos) was a valuable ally to the Franks in their campaign against the Moors in the region, and was granted the title of Count of the area bordering on the Arab part of Spain. No sooner were the Moors dealt with, than the pugnacious Normans arrived in their longboats and Wilfred's skill on the battlefield was once more put to the test. Finally, as he lay mortally wounded, his feudal lord and leader of the Franks, Charles the Bald, was so distressed that he dipped his fingers in brave Wilfred's gaping wound and drew four bloody stripes on his hitherto plain yellow shield. "These shall be your colours from this day forth, most valiant Wilfred!" said Charles – or words to that effect. By the time the warrior Guifre died in AD 897, the earldom of Barcelona, the Catalan alliance and the Catalan flag had come into existence. So much for that colourful historical fact.

In the centuries that followed, no new friends or foes of note arrived on the coast – except for a few bloodthirsty pirates from as far afield as Turkey and Algeria. Now it was the turn of the Catalans themselves to build ships and set off eastwards, hitting first on the Balearic Islands, then reaching Sardinia and Sicily. They took control of Naples and held the city for a considerable time. It must have been a period of good

fortune and prosperity, since the Catalans on the Costa Brava to this day still hark back with pride to this glorious era whenever they wish to pour scorn on the achievements of the government in Madrid. Yes, that's correct, there is no love lost between the inhabitants of this corner of the country and the rest of Spain. For the simple reason that the Catalan does not consider himself a Spaniard. Spaniards are those who, towards the end of the Middle Ages, managed to gain the upper hand in Catalonia by means of tactical marriages among throne heirs. From a Catalan point of view, history could sound something like this: after the Normans came the Spaniards…

To cut a long story short, it was not long before the French arrived and later the British took an interest in the area. Any plans they might have had were nipped in the bud by the French during the Napoleonic Wars.

All the various peoples who have come and gone and thereby shaped the history of the Costa Brava over the last two millennia must surely have had good reasons for doing so. Certainly many of these have to do with questions of strategy and power politics. But underlying all these was probably the simple fact that they were intoxicated by the sheer beauty of the coast; the bays, the mountains, the fertile hinterland, the riches of the sea and of course the majestic Pyrenees to the north, reaching right down to the shoreline. Each conquering power has left its mark on the landscape: Iberians, Greeks, Romans, Goths and

Arabs, the Normans less so. They generally burnt down whatever they found. The Franks, too and the Spaniards of old left us many traces of their cultures which are among today's most beautiful treasures.

How can the ugliness of certain parts of today's Costa Brava be explained? Industrialization spread of course, though was concentrated mainly in cities, such as Barcelona and Girona. Maybe it was when Catalan poet Ferran Agullo, overwhelmed by the beauty of his homeland, coined the phrase "Costa Brava" almost 100 years ago. The stretch of coast between Portbou in the north down almost as far as Barcelona has become the most famous on the Mediterranean, perhaps in the world: Costa Brava – the wild coast. So began the most important period – ecologically and economically – in Catalan history.

The first peaceful "invaders" were the artists, fascinated by the landscape and the light. They were, if you like, the first tourists. Picasso, Dalí, their wives and friends came; Miró and Gaudí were here already. Each artist began his own personal dialogue with the landscape and created a style which was synonymous with the Costa Brava, to an extent comparable with, say Van Gogh and Provence. The Costa Brava served not merely as subject matter, but rather as the source of their fantasy and inspiration – then, as now, fertile terrain for the creative mind. In the evenings they would sit in dimly lit bars, fisherman and artist side by side, each regarding the other as slightly mad, but drinking companions all the same. It would be impossible to conjure up such an atmosphere today – the drinking perhaps – but not this off-beat, good-natured and always respectful camaraderie.

This period, during which the first (intellectual) summer guests started arriving, when the money to be made out of them was a pittance, mere pocket-money compared to the undreamed-of gold-rush atmosphere of the 1960s, was literally the calm before the storm – it was too good to last. The next crisis tore the country apart, when Spaniards turned this time on their fellow countrymen. The Spanish Civil War of 1936–39 cost one million lives. Catalans maintain it was not a civil war as such, but an invasion by Spanish Fascists, supporters of General Franco – just one of a succession of attempts by the Spaniards to subjugate Catalonia over the centuries.

Barcelona – heart and mind of Catalan resistance – was particularly badly hit. The city had to defend itself not only against the bombs and artillery fire of the external enemy, but was also torn apart by an internal power struggle amongst social democrats, anarchists, Trotzkyists, Soviet communists and commissars, who alternately fought against each other, only to join forces later against the all-powerful Falange troops who were supported by the German Luftwaffe. Volunteers from many European nations fought alongside the Catalans for the cause of freedom. The names Orwell and Hemmingway immediately spring to mind, although this would not do justice to the many other nameless heroes of that

La Boqueria

Barcelona's famous market hall on the Rambla, also known as Mercat de Sant Josep, is without doubt one of the most attractive and colourful markets in Europe. There was a livestock market here as early as the 16th century – Boqueria comes from "boc", the Catalan and Provençal word for billy goat. In 1835, the neighbouring Carmelite nunnery Sant Josep was demolished as part of a general secularization process, and in its place the grandiose market hall was erected in the neoclassical style. Over 800 stalls make for a unique atmosphere. Look out for Pinocho's stand (his real name is Joan Bayen) and let yourself be tempted by his Catalan specialities amidst the hustle and bustle all around you.

time. Barcelona, that great city port – held then by many supposedly "civilized" Europeans to be on a par with Africa – became an isolated pocket of resistance to Fascism in Europe.

History has shown us few examples of moral justice and made no exception here: as so often, Goliath triumphed over David. In 1939 Franco's army overcame long and dogged resistance and marched into Barcelona. With her fell Catalonia. The victors were merciless in avenging their dead, quite in keeping with their motto, "Viva la muerte!" – "Long live death!" As many as 50 civilians were singled out each day, condemned as enemies of the people and executed. Thousands were incarcerated in prisoner-of-war camps, streets were renamed in Spanish, Catalan monuments replaced as a rule by statues of Franco, the "heroic Generalissimo". This brutal policy of forcing the Catalans into line had as its watchword, "A united Spain needs no regionalism". Language too was a target under Franco's repressive regime: "Speak like a Christian!" he ordered, which of course meant speak Spanish, i.e.

Castilian. More than 25 Catalan-language newspapers were banned, their owners either dispossessed or forced to publish in Castilian. Catalan was no longer taught as a subject in schools. No effort was spared on the part of the victors systematically to destroy the centuries-old culture of Catalonia. However they did not succeed. The death of Franco on 20 November 1975 marks the resurrection of Catalonia, so to speak. On 11 September 1977, the Catalan national holiday *Diada*, more than one million demonstrators gathered in Barcelona to demand Catalan autonomy. Two years later, their wish was granted.

Back to the Costa Brava. Soon after World War II, a slow but steady influx of people began – on a huge scale. They came from all corners of Europe, virtually simultaneously, from France, the Benelux states, England, Scandinavia and, above all, Germany. Like the ancient Greeks and the Franks before them, all of these people were after the same things: sun, sea and sand – and fun. Despite their not exactly rosy financial prospects, they

Bellcaire d'Empordà with the Pyrenean massif in the background

vowed to come again the following year. There was no way round it: parts of the Costa Brava sacrificed their beauty for the sake of accommodating their guests. Whole new resorts sprang up almost overnight, one high-rise hotel after the other, holiday villages splattered across hillsides. The wheels of the Catalan economy spun faster and faster to keep pace with demand. Look at Lloret, or better still Platja d'Aro, which in summer has over 100,000 inhabitants. You would have to look very hard to find a 40-year-old who was actually born here. Until 45 years ago there was nothing but the beach, the sun and the mountains – all guaranteed to get you hooked, either on the great outdoors or on the money you could make exploiting it. There is an old fisherman in Lloret whose impoverished grandfather emigrated to South America, where he ended his days a luckless gold panner. His grandson, on the other hand, stayed put and struck it rich, selling the family's land to property developers eager for somewhere to build their colossal hotel blocks. Now a millionaire, he occasionally watches from a distance as the remaining fishermen sit mending their nets.

Alternatively, he heads north, where there are still more of his ex-colleagues, takes a room in a small B&B and sits back to enjoy the view across one of the fantastic bays. With the trained eye and instinct of a successful businessman, he wonders how much money is waiting to be made here. Wouldn't it be possible to attract the kind of noble clientele you see on the Côte d'Azur, make it a paradise for the rich and famous? But this time making sure not to let in any old Tom, Dick or Harry!

Such thoughts cross his mind from time to time and it's quite possible that, sitting at that café in Cadaqués, the feel of a dog's nose or the sound of a moped will drag him back to reality. Maybe he'll notice the pale, moonlit façades of the old houses, hear the gentle lapping of the waves. For this is reality. The simple truth.

History at a glance

5000 BC
First stone-age settlements

218 BC
The Romans conquer the Iberian peninsula

49 BC
Julius Caesar in Barcelona

AD 419
The Visigoths invade northern Spain and Barcelona, calling the territory "Gotalonia"

988
Barcelona granted independence

1137
Unification of the kingdoms of Catalonia and Aragón

1212–35
King Jaime I of Aragón conquers the Balearic Islands. Catalonia remains the dominant force in the western Mediterranean until well into the 14th century

1469
Ferdinand II, heir apparent in Aragón, marries Isabella, heiress to the throne in Castile, thereby uniting the two kingdoms

1492
Christopher Columbus discovers America. The king receives him on his return to Spain, in the royal palace in Barcelona

1641
Revolt against the Spaniards in Barcelona, which is suppressed only after ten years

1714
End of War of Spanish Succession. Since Catalonia sided with the Habsburgs, Catalan is banned, as a punishment

1859
The Renaixena movement signifies the call for more cultural independence for Catalonia

1888
First World's Fair in Barcelona

c. 1900
Beginnings of tourist trade on the Costa Brava

1931
Second Spanish Republic is declared. Catalonia is granted longed-for autonomy

1936
Start of Spanish Civil War. Catalan autonomy is revoked

1939
End of the Civil War sees one million dead. Catalonia practically ceases to exist

1975
Franco dies. Juan Carlos is crowned king

1977
First free parliamentary elections

1979
Catalonia regains its autonomy

1986
Spain joins the then European Community

1992
Barcelona stages the summer Olympic Games, with venues along the Costa Brava

Moors, artists and Sardana

Catalonia has a culture all its own: a cursory look at the Costa Brava

Arabs

The invasion by the Moors of the Iberian peninsula presented a great threat to the empire of the Visigoths who ruled Spain for almost 300 years. By AD 711, the region around the Costa Brava was firmly in Arab hands. The Moorish advance seemed unstoppable and took them over the border into France. It was not until 732 that they were halted by Charles Martell, Regent at the Franconian court, in an encounter near Poitiers. The Moors brought a highly developed culture to Catalonia, but they were unable to keep control of the region for very long. Charlemagne succeeded in winning back bit by bit the area between Barcelona and Girona in the period from 795 to 811, establishing thereby the so-called Spanish March, a kind of buffer zone separating the Moslems from the Christians. The border with the remainder of Moorish Spain ran just south of Barcelona for several centuries.

Boats

On most beaches along the Costa Brava it is possible to rent various kinds of boats. *Patines* (pedalos) and *gondolas* (one- and two-man boats propelled using paddles), for example. Be careful though not to venture too far from the beach, since the currents can be strong and unpredictable, making it almost impossible to get back to the shore. Watch out, too, for the breakers in the rocky coves. The surging waves are more than a match for the *gondolas*, which tend to capsize easily. Some hotels rent out sailing dinghies to experienced sailors.

Borbón

The Spanish royal family. King Don Juan Carlos de Borbón y Borbón has been on the throne since the death of General Franco in 1975, and is head of state within a parliamentary democracy. Juan Carlos is a descendant of the Spanish branch of the French ruling dynasty, the Bourbons. His father was Earl of Barcelona.

"Casa Batlló" by Gaudí in Barcelona is a typically fantastic product of Catalan art

Corrida

Bullfighting, the bloody, Sunday pastime of the Spanish people, also takes place on the Costa Brava between spring (after Easter) and autumn (September). Apart from in Barcelona, however, bullfights do not draw such large crowds as in Castile or Andalusia, for example. In fact there is a growing feeling in Catalonia that bullfighting is nothing more than a cruel bloodsport, and Tossa de Mar on the Costa Brava has gone so far as to ban the Corrida, the first town in Spain to do so.

Monumental painting at the Dalí Museum in Figueres

Dalí

In his own humble opinion, he was "the greatest artist in the world". Salvador Dalí was born in Figueres in 1904, the son of a Catalan notary. In 1929 the already world-famous Surrealist painter moved, with his wife Gala, to the birthplace of his fa-

ther, Port Lligat near Cadaqués. In contrast to other artists, Dalí did not flee into exile during the Franco dictatorship, but remained in his Catalan homeland and carried on working. He was revered by the dictator as a great artist. For these reasons, he was much criticized during his lifetime. Dalí considered himself to be Catalan through and through, though this did not prevent him from bequeathing a large proportion of his life's work to the Spanish state – much to the annoyance of the Catalan government. Consequently, many of his pictures are on display only in Madrid, and not in the perhaps more fitting surroundings of the Dalí Museum in Figueres.

Eisler

Catalonia's capital, Barcelona, had applied to host the Olympic Games in 1936, a privilege that was eventually granted to Berlin. As a protest against this decision, plans were made to hold an "Olimpíada Popular", as a kind of gesture of peace. The German composer Hanns Eisler had already written the official anthem for the games, which were due to start on 19 July 1939, but in the night of 18 July, the outbreak of the Spanish Civil War stopped all thoughts of peace in their tracks.

Flamenco

As you would expect, this dance is high on the cultural agenda in the tourist centres of the Costa Brava, as *the* typical Spanish dance form. However it is not really part of Catalan tradition. True flamenco is a form of music and dance probably of Arab origin and handed down by gypsies, picking up Jewish influences on the way. It originated in Andalusia and it is here – and only here (with the exception of Madrid and Barcelona) – that you will find flamenco being celebrated in its original and most passionate form. Each performance is unique in its drama and emotion, the mood of both participants and spectators – even the level of alcohol that has been consumed – being the decisive factors in the spectacle. Don't expect anything like this in the night clubs and folklore evenings on the Costa Brava. Here, it's little more than a gimmick to attract tourists.

Gaudí

Antoni Gaudí, the most famous Catalan architect, was born in Reus in 1852. He was the true master of that highly imaginative Art Nouveau typical of Barcelona. His masterpieces include the residential and commercial buildings on the Passeig de Gràcia, Güell Park and of course the Sagrada Família, the bizarre Modernist cathedral in Barcelona. Construction work began over 100 years ago and an end is still not yet in sight. The church is nevertheless considered to be one of the most significant sacred buildings in the world. Antoni Gaudí died in Barcelona in 1926, knocked down by a tram.

Greeks

The Ancient Greeks turned their attention to the Costa Brava early on. About 6 BC they founded the settlement Palaiopolis, which was extended some 100 years later to form the much larger Neopolis. The Greeks were succeeded by the Romans, who re-named the entire site Empúries, taken from

Statue of a Greek god among the ruins at Empúries

the Greek word *emporion*, which means trading centre. The ruins can be seen to this day. The fishing port Roses can trace its origins back to the Greeks; settlers from Rhodes arrived there in 6 BC, calling their colony Rhode, a name that has mutated over the centuries to become Roses.

Iberians

The Iberians were the pre-indogermanic population of Spain. They also built settlements on the Costa Brava. Their Iron Age relics bear witness to this fact today. Experts have succeeded in deciphering their script; their spoken language, however, remains a mystery. About 6 BC the Iberian peoples began intermingling with the Celts who were migrating across the Pyrenees from the north. The

Celtiberians were subsequently overrun by Phoenicians, Greeks and Romans.

Catalan

The language of the Costa Brava, though the Catalan people speak Spanish (Castilian) too, of course. Catalan developed from Vulgar Latin. Its various dialects can be heard from southern France down to Valencia, on the Balearic Islands and even in Alghero on Sardinia. Place names on the Costa Brava are indicated both in Catalan and Castilian. You are more than likely to see the following slogan daubed on house walls, "Catalunya no es Espanya!" There can be no mistaking where you are!

Mandíbula

Evidence of the earliest settlements in Catalonia: the remains of human jaw bones were discovered near Banyoles in 1887. They have been identified as pre-Neandertal, making them more than 100,000 years old.

Miró

The second Catalan artist to achieve worldwide fame in the 20th century. Joan Miró was born in 1893, the son of a goldsmith and watchmaker in Montroig near Barcelona. His paintings, lithographs and sculptures have made an unforgettable contribution to the modern art scene. One of his most famous pieces is *Sunbird*, a sculpture in bronze from the late 1940s. Miró's works – especially in poster form – find buyers the world over, although many are probably not quite sure what they are buying! His colour composition, the eccentric, lively forms and shapes have made accessible the world of modern art to many who had hitherto not had a clue about contemporary artistic forms. His credo was that the most important thing was to bear your soul. Joan Miró died at the age of 90 in 1983 at his retirement home on Mallorca.

National parks

Now that the original building boom on the Costa Brava has more or less subsided, and the need to protect the environment is increasingly being felt in Spain, several significant national parks have been established. The most important is *Aiguamolls de l'Empordà*, its 5,000 hectares being one of the largest wetland habitats in Spain. This expanse of marshland in Empordà, to the west of the Gulf of Roses, is a vital stopover for migratory birds. Even flamingos and storks can be observed here. More information can be obtained in El Cortalet, on the road between Sant Pere Pescador and Castelló d'Empúries.

The *Medes Islands* lie off the coast at L'Estartit and are an underwater paradise, boasting rare flora and fauna. The coral reefs here are home to almost 600 species of sea creature. The many underwater grottoes and caves are an ideal spot to find even large fish, such as eels, dogfish and various types of ray.

The national park around the *Serra de Montseny*, between Barcelona and Girona, is densely forested and covers an area of 30,000 hectares, a suitable habitat for wildcats and wild boar. For more information about the park, contact the education centre at Can Massaguer.

Orwell

The author of the famous novel *1984* was born Eric A. Blair, but is best known under his pseudonym George Orwell. He came to Barcelona in 1936 as a newspaper reporter and began his novel *Homage to Catalonia* – his best work, in his opinion – several months later. During the Spanish Civil War, he fought as a corporal in the POUM militia of the Marxist worker's party. In May 1937 he was wounded and secretely fled to France four weeks later with his wife.

Peralada

Catalan wine-growing region to the northeast of Figueres. The area has turned more recently to producing very fine dry white wines, which go particularly well with fish, mussels and other shellfish caught off the Costa Brava. Be sure to try the Perelada sparkling white wine, which the Spaniards generously term *champàn*.

Pyrenees

High mountain range in northern Catalonia, the foothills running directly down to the sea on the Costa Brava. Some 400 km in length and 100 km wide, the Pyrenees stretch from the Atlantic to the Mediterranean, separating the Iberian peninsula from the rest of the European continent. The highest peak is the 3,404-m-high Pico de Aneto. On the southern face of the Pyrenees between France and Spain lies the miniature state of Andorra, where Catalan is the official language. A day trip from Figueres.

Ramblas

Tree-lined avenues common to most places on the Costa Brava.

They originally followed dried-up river beds and were used as simple footpaths. Now they are a focal point of the community, especially in the evenings. Here, rich or poor, you can see and be seen and quench your thirst. The most famous is of course in Barcelona. No trip to the Costa Brava is complete without a stroll down it.

Drugs

Certainly just as big a problem as anywhere else in Europe. Perhaps Spain suffers more though, since it is here that the main routes by which drugs enter Europe from South America come together. The Barrio Chino (Chinese Quarter) in Barcelona is a magnet for addicts and dealers alike, as are several other tourist destinations on the Costa Brava.

Sardana

The traditional folk dance of Catalonia and the Costa Brava. Monuments have even been erected in its honour, in Lloret de Mar and on the Montjuïc in Barcelona, for example. The "stage" is often just a square or the middle of the road. Accompanied by various pipes and wind instruments, complete strangers join hands and begin to dance this combination of long and short steps in the round, new dancers joining in all the time. There is no stamping of feet or flamboyant gestures, just a quiet sense of oneness and intimacy that unites the Catalan peoples, a physical demonstration of what sets them apart. This is presumably the reason why Franco banned the Sardana in 1939. If an outsider tries to join in, the cir-

The closed formation of the Sardana dancers symbolizes unity

cle opens to welcome him, in acknowledgement of his desire to better understand the Catalan mentality.

Separatism
Until his death in 1975, Franco's central government in Madrid systematically suppressed Catalonia. This traumatic experience, with its centuries-old origins, can still be felt today. The Catalans have of course achieved a large degree of autonomy, having their own provincial government, president and occasional state visits; a status similar to the Basques. They can openly and freely cultivate their language and culture. And yet, these facts have done little to contain the groundswell of desire for a truly independent Catalonia. On the contrary, the actions of extreme separatists have, on occasions, been violent, including bombings and assassination attempts. Security experts suspect that the Basque terrorist organization ETA has even given logistical aid.

Siesta
Every visitor to Spain is strongly advised to take up this Spanish custom and escape the heat of the midday sun. Peace descends on public life (except in restaurants and bars) at around 1 pm and lasts until between 4 and 5 pm. When in Rome ... as they say.

Tramontana
Fierce north wind blowing down the Costa Brava from the mountains, generally in spring and autumn, and lasting between three and four days. It famously whips up the sea and people's tempers! The Catalans say, with a knowing look, that the Tramontana can drive you mad. It also features in regional literature, not as a feared natural phenomenon, but rather as a creative, passionate force.

18

Ulbricht

The German communist and one-time GDR head of state Walter Ulbricht was a political activist in the Spanish Civil War. He was responsible for monitoring the loyalty to the party demonstrated by German brigade members, volunteers fighting against Franco's Falange forces. Some historians lay part of the blame at Ulbricht's feet for the street fighting in Barcelona in 1937 in which anarchists, Trotzkyists and soviet-oriented communists fought against each other – at a cost of more than 1,000 lives.

Villa Olímpica

The Olympic Village in Barcelona is seen in the whole of Catalonia as a symbol of economic strength, modernity and independence. A whole new district – and a magnet for tourists – was created, boasting a promenade, a beach, a marina and a daring 44-storey hotel, Arts, supposedly the most luxurious in Europe. As is typical for the Costa Brava the roads and rail tracks that originally ran along the coastline have been re-routed underground. Barcelona, with its more than 2 million inhabitants, has gained a quiet, yet urban attraction, which offers the visitor the chance to relax and enjoy himself.

Volcanoes

The volcanic landscape *La Garrotxa*, between Banyoles and Olot, is one of the most fascinating in Europe. More than 40 extinct craters lie scattered over a beautiful, mountainous landscape. Right in the middle lies the medieval village Sant Pau, with its charming square ringed by arcades. This is an ideal base

for walks through the Garrotxa, the land of the dormant volcanoes. For more information, contact the *Centre d'Iniciatives Turístiques, Edifici Plaça del Mercat; Tel. 972 26 01 41*

Economy

The autonomous region of Catalonia (including the provinces of Girona, Barcelona, Lleida and Tarragona) has a population of approximately 7 million, roughly half of whom live in and around Barcelona. Catalonia is the most important economic region in Spain (yielding 20 per cent of the gross national product) with car manufacture in Barcelona and the chemicals industry in Tarragona. A particularly lucrative source of revenue is tourism (approximately 12 million holidaymakers per year). In addition, the fishing industry (e.g. in Roses and L'Escala) and agriculture still play a vital role. Besides tomatoes, olives and fruit, wine is a major product, especially in the area Empurdà-Costa Brava between Roses and Cadaqués and also to the south of Barcelona.

X

Very common letter in the Catalan language. For example, *xocolata* (chocolate), *cotxa* (car). The "x" is pronounced "sh" – hence shokolata, cotsha.

Zamorra

In the bars of the Costa Brava, which are particularly popular amongst football fans, the name Ricardo Zamorra, "the cat", is still widely heard. The most famous Spanish goalkeeper of all time is a Catalan folk hero. He played in the 1930s for Barcelona FC.

Culinary pot-pourri of unusual recipes

Costa Brava cuisine: a captivating combination of seemingly incompatible ingredients

Dining on the Costa Brava? The gourmet turns his nose up in distaste at the seemingly endless chain of hot-dog and fish'n'chip snack bars with which the concrete jungles of Calella or Lloret are so well endowed. There's no denying the fact that these emporia of bad taste do exist, but it would be to do local Catalan cuisine a disservice if you were to lump it together with the fast-food fry-ups that are so typical of catering for masses of tourists. On the contrary, you will find a variety on the menu here that is only seldom found in the rest of Spain and that can be rightly compared to the culinary achievements on the other side of the border with France. This is hardly surprising, since French and Italian influences abound, as a conse-quence of Catalonia's historical significance for the western Mediterranean. A further con-tributory factor is the rich variety of fresh produce avail-able, a tempting source of ingre-dients from which cooks and chefs can choose – the key to good cooking. The finest fish and all manner of shellfish from local waters, trout from the crystal-clear Pyrenean streams, game from the forests and fresh salads, vegetables and fruit from local farms and gardens. All this rounded off with superb wines and pure mineral water. So far, so good.

What singles out Catalan cuisine in particular, however, is the traditional combination of ingredients that on the face of it do not seem to go together at all: chopped onions and almonds, crayfish with chicken, goose accompanied by turnips and pears, sugar in black pudding. Initial reactions range from curiosity to utter

Plenty to choose from on one of the Costa Brava's many markets

disbelief, but do give these excellent local specialities a try – they taste terrific. Don't just play it safe with paella, gazpacho or calamares coated in breadcrumbs.

For the locals, breakfast usually means just a cup of milky coffee and a croissant, more often than not in a small café round the corner. Here you will find those specialities that are particular to Spain: *bocadillos*, sandwiches, and, of course, *tapas*, those little appetizers that, don't forget, can be combined to make an excellent meal. Here are a few more suggestions to whet your appetite: air-dried Serrano ham, meatballs, sardines that have been fried or marinated in vinegar, oil and garlic. Or what about calves' kidneys in sherry, mussels cooked in the oven, potato salad, marinated cockles, diverse omelettes *(tortillas)*, sandwiches with crab and mayonnaise, prawns cooked in oil *(gambas)*, chick-peas with tomatoes, mild pepperoni with olives, wrapped in anchovies *(anxova)*, marinated squid, salted almonds, various types of sausage, etc. Such delicacies are hard to resist, especially when the days are long and one's appetite is correspondingly larger!

Traditionally, the main meal of the day is the evening meal, a good opportunity to succumb to a few Catalan temptations. For starters, in addition to *tapas*, there are various soups (especially fish), sausage (such as black pudding with sugar, *botifarra*) or a portion of prawns with *allioli*, home-made garlic mayonnaise. As a starter you may be offered *pa amb tomàquet*, a piece of toasted bread, coated in olive oil and with crushed tomato on top.

To follow, you could try some fish dishes, for example, fresh sole, grilled sardines with some salad, *arròs negre* (rice with black squid sauce), *zarzuela* (stew made of fish, mussels and prawns), *simitomba* (stew made of fish, potatoes and garlic), *suquet de peix* (monkfish with potatoes), *rascassa al forn* (scorpion fish baked in the oven), or *llagosta amb pollastre* (crayfish with chicken). The portions are usually so generous that you might be inclined to forego the second main course – but that would really be a shame, when faced with a choice of *pollastre amb musclos* (chicken with mussels), *ànec amb naps* (duck with turnips), *mongetes amb botifarra* (stew made of broad beans and

Mealtimes

It takes some getting used to perhaps, but here on the Costa Brava, as in the rest of Spain, meals are taken at totally different times than in the rest of Europe. Lunch seldom begins before 1 pm, usually at around 2 pm, sometimes even at 3 pm. It's hardly surprising, then, that the main meal never starts before 8.30 pm, but more likely between 9 pm and 10 pm.

Beach restaurants offer tempting fresh fish and fine wines

sweet black pudding), *cuixa de xai amb herbes* (leg of lamb with herbs), *pit d'ànec amb salsa de brandy i trufes* (breast of duck with brandy-truffle sauce). To accompany these dishes, you'll find *escalivada* (warm vegetables), *past's d'albergínies* (aubergine pudding) or *fideuà* (Catalan vermicelli with garlic and saffron).

You wish an excellent dessert? How about this for choice: *ensaïmada* (ring-shaped yeast cakes fried in oil), *panellets* (Catalan macaroons) and of course the famous *crema catalana*, or flan, a creamy mixture of eggs and milk, coated with a layer of warm caramel.

Drinks

Catalonia is wine country. Good quality, light, dry white and sparkling wines have been produced here for many years. The principal growing areas are Alella, Empordà and Penedès, which lies further to the south. The best red wines come from Priorat, Sitges and Alt-Empordà. When dining out, it is customary to order a bottle of mineral water, either carbonated *(con gaz)* or noncarbonated *(sin gaz).* The wine list will also include *sangría*, a kind of punch made of red wine, fruit and a generous dash of cognac. This is most typically drunk by tourists, but, if served ice cold and watered down with mineral water, is not a bad thirst-quencher on hot evenings. Catalonia's light sparkling wines, the *cavas*, are becoming increasingly popular and are indeed of excellent quality.

Coffee on the Costa Brava is generally very good indeed. In the morning, breakfast is washed down with *café con leche*, a milky coffee, similar to the French *café au lait*. In the afternoon and evening, *café solo* is preferred, comparable to an espresso. Or alternatively a *café cortado* (with just a hint of milk) or *café carajillo* (with a dash of cognac). Another Costa Brava speciality is *horchata de chufa*, an ice-cold almond milk drink.

Leather, fashion, junk

A shopping spree in the shops, boutiques and markets offers something for every pocket

The days when Spain was a cheap holiday destination are well and truly over. Retail prices on the Costa Brava and in Barcelona are comparable with those in northern Europe, and in some cases are even higher. The coastal resorts also offer a selection of typical shops along the promenade, selling nothing but junk that really isn't worth buying. So what should you bring back as a souvenir?

Barcelona is a shopper's paradise – especially if money is no object. It pays to wander through the shops and boutiques; Barcelona is one of the top fashion centres in the world, alongside Milan, Rome, Paris, New York and Tokyo. If you have a good grasp of the Catalan language, you should venture into the flea market, Mercat gòtic d'antiguitats, on the Plaça de Pi and Plaça Sant Josep Oriol, where you're sure to find some fine souvenirs. Antiques fans should head for the Bulevard des Antiquaris on the Passeig de Gràcia 55–57 (especially for Barcelona's Art Nouveau) and the small antique

Catalan sparkling wine: the cavas are of the highest quality

shops in the old part of town, particularly on the Banys Nous.

Inexpensive souvenirs are, for example, wine and cognac; the latter is particularly cheap here. High-quality shoes and leather goods are also worth looking at, as are items made of hemp, such as *alpargatas*, cheap summer shoes.

Keep a lookout for the numerous ceramics shops, which can be found in most places on the Costa Brava. It pays to have a good look around, since in addition to the usual junk on offer, you will also find attractive and reasonably priced items. La Bisbal is the centre of the ceramics industry.

Markets

Self-caterers can find everything they need on the many weekly markets dotted around the region. Here is a list of the most important of them, arranged according to the day on which they are held: Monday *(Blanes, Cadaqués, Torroella de Montgrí)*, Tuesday *(Lloret de Mar, Palamós)*, Wednesday *(Llançà)*, Thursday *(L'Estartit, Tossa de Mar)*, Friday *(Platja d'Aro, Port de la Selva)*, Saturday *(Girona)*, Sunday *(L'Escala, Roses, Sant Feliu de Guíxols)*. The markets in *Barcelona* are open daily.

Fiestas and festivals

*Dances and processions abound
all year round*

The Spaniards, as a nation, really know how to have a good time; this is, after all, the home of the fiesta! Most festivals are of religious significance. Add to these the numerous bullfights, which take place from Easter to October on Sundays and public holidays, from 5 pm or 6 pm. There's always something to celebrate.

PUBLIC HOLIDAYS

Offices, banks and many shops remain closed on these days.

1 January *Año Nuevo (New Year's Day)*
6 January *Los Reyes Magos (Epiphany)*
Holy Week *Viernes Santo (Good Friday)*
Easter Monday *Lunes de Pascua*
1 May *Día del Trabajo (Labour Day)*
24 June *San Juan (St John, name day of the king)*
15 August *Asunción de la Virgen (Assumption)*
11 September *Diada Nacional de Catalunya (Catalan National Holiday)*
24 September *Festa Major de la Mercè (Patron saint of Barcelona; holiday here only)*

The popular giant figures at the "Festa Major de la Mercè"

12 October *Día de la Hispanidad (Discovery of America)*
1 November *Todos los Santos (All Saints' Day)*
6 December *Día de la Constitución (Constitution Day)*
8 December *Inmaculada Concepción* (Immaculate Conception)
25/26 December *Navidad (Christmas Day)*

SPECIAL EVENTS

January
Fira de Joguines – toy fair with street parties in Barcelona, 1 to 5 January

February
Skiing championships in the Pyrenees (La Molina)
Carnival in Barcelona, Girona and other towns and cities (banned during Franco era)

March/April
★Viernes Santo, major *Holy Week celebrations* in Girona. In some towns, a "dance of death" is performed by spectators dressed as skeletons. The *Passion plays* in Verges are well worth seeing. *Traditional pilgrimage* in Barcelona to the chapel of St Medir in the district of Gràcia

April

Agriculture and Industry Trade Fair in the trade and industry centre in Figueres, with bullfighting, art exhibitions and *Jocs Florals*, a revival of medieval poetry competition
Sant Jordi (23 April) – the famous triple holiday in Barcelona: St George's Day (patron saint of Catalonia), Festival of the Rose and Book Festival (anniversary of Cervantes's death). *Feria de Abril* – Andalusian festival in Barcelona, celebrated by migrants from the south

May

Flower Show in San Pedro de Galligans monastery in Girona
Eudaldo Market in Ripoll
Sant Ponç with alternative herb market in Barcelona (Carrer Hospital)

June

Folklore Fair in Palamós
Sardana Festival and *waterski competition* in Sant Pere Pescador
Folklore Fair in Tossa de Mar
★ *Nit de Sant Joan* (23 June) – Barcelona marks Midsummer's Eve with an exuberant festival

July

★ *Aplec*, huge Sardana *feria* in Olot (more than 5,000 dancers take part)
Music Festival in Calonge in medieval castle
16 July: ★ *Mare de Déu del Carme* – floating processions off almost all the fishing villages along the Costa Brava, *Cristina Fairs* in Lloret, Blanes, Sant Cristina d'Aro, Portbou, Sant Feliu de Guíxols, L'Estartit

---

MARCO POLO SELECTION: FESTIVALS

1 Mercè in Barcelona
In honour of the patron saint in September. Two-day party during which the city goes crazy (page 29)

2 Nit de Sant Joan
Exuberant Midsummer's-Eve parties in most towns (page 28)

3 Aplec
Major Sardana dance festival in Olot. Over 5,000 dance until well after midnight (page 28)

4 Viernes Santo
Holy Week celebrations with "dance of death" performed by spectators in skeleton costumes: strange and unearthly. Most impressive in Girona and Verges (page 27)

5 Mare de Déu del Carme
Colourful, floating fishermen's processions. Don't miss the Cristina Festival in Lloret de Mar. Fishing boats head for the bay with the Cristina chapel (page 28)

6 The International Music Festival in Sant Feliu de Guíxols
Featuring the most popular stars of the concert scene. Be sure to get your tickets early! (page 29)

Zarzuela

Culinary treat on the Costa Brava: Catalan stew made with fish, squid, prawns and mussels. It is best eaten in the better-known fish restaurants, where it is at its freshest. Zarzuela also has another meaning: Spanish operetta.

Music Festival in Torroella de Montgrí
Music Festival at Castell d'Aro
Teatre Grec – Barcelona's international theatre festival

August

St Dominic Festival in Pals
★ *International Music Festival* in Sant Feliu de Guíxols
Folklore Festival in Llançà and Platja d'Aro
International Music Festival in Cadaqués
Festa Major de Gràcia – colourful festival in Barcelona's Gràcia district, great atmosphere

September

Festival with Sardana dancing in L'Escala
Fair with Sardana dancing in Cadaqués
Patron saint's festival in Olot
Festival in Lloret de Mar
★ *Festa Major de la Mercè* – the festival to end all festivals in Barcelona: the city goes wild
Festa Major in Besalú
Rice Festival in Palafrugell
Art exhibition in Palamós
Wine Festival in Llançà

October

Day of the Sea with floating procession in Sant Feliu de Guíxols
St Narcissus Festival in Girona, featuring bullfighting and equestrian shows
Start of the *opera season* in the Gran Teatre del Liceu in Barcelona, newly restored following the fire in 1994
Patron saint's festival in Girona, end of the month

November

Catalina Festival in Torroella de Montgrí – another Sardana highlight
Agricultural Trade Fair in Banyoles

December

Fira de Santa Llúcia, pre-Christmas nativity market in Barcelona – everything from kitsch to fine art
Festa de Santa Llúcia in L'Estartit

Part of every folklore festival: traditional Catalan costumes and music

SHORT TOUR

(112–113/C–E3–5) Host to the Olympic Games in 1992, Barcelona is one of the most attractive cities in the Mediterranean. The city is famous for the brilliant Art Nouveau artist Gaudí, its extravagant zest for life, football, bacchanalian markets and pickpockets. It is the capital of modern design and a fashion mecca. Have we forgotten anything on our list of superlatives? See for yourselves the urban heart of Catalonia with its 2 million inhabitants! Sample the view from the fortress on top of Montjuïc (also the site of the Olympic stadium), which can be reached by cable car from the harbour. Or from the amusement park Tibidabo in the west, or the viewing platform of the column erected in honour of Columbus, which stands at the lower end of the Rambla.

SIGHTS

☛ **City Map inside back cover**

Ajuntament   (U/D4)
Old Town Hall (Casa de la Ciutat) with inner courtyard and magnificent chambers. Built from 1369 to 1378; its neoclassical façade dates from 1840. *Plaça de Sant Jaume*

Catedral de Santa Eulalia   (U/D3)
Barcelona's Gothic cathedral. It took from 1298 to 1458 to build and is situated in the old part of town on the site of two early Christian basilicas. The stained-glass windows are some 500 years old. *Plaça de la Seu*

Gaudí
The brilliant Catalan architect Antoni Gaudí (1852–1926) bestowed Barcelona with many of its most striking architectural features, exemplifying Modernism (Catalan Art Nouveau). Here, the most significant, which should not be missed: *Museu Gaudí* (**O**), which contains drawings, sketches and furniture in the architect's last residence. Adjacent to the *Parc Güell* (**O**), a park featuring spectacular buildings and open spaces, encompassed by a colourful serpentine balustrade. *Passeig de Gràcia* (**U/C2–3, D3**), a magnificent boulevard lined with impressive Gaudí residences, such as Casa Batlló (43) and Casa Milà (92). *Sagrada Família* (**U/D1**), Gaudí's unfinished masterpiece, world-famous symbol of Barcelona. Cathedral with bizarre towers and intriguing sculptures inspired by nature, in accordance with the Gaudí motto: "Architecture must grow!" Work began on the structure at the end of the 19th century and continues to this day, financed solely by private donations to preserve a sense of closeness to ordinary parishioners. *Carrer de Mallorca*

Columbus's column   (U/D4)
☝ In April 1493 Columbus returned from his first voyage to America. The Catholic monarchs Isabella and Ferdinand received him with great pomp on his arrival in Barcelona. It was not until 1888, however, that this 66-m-high column was erected at the end of the Rambla in honour of the great explorer. Take the lift (a tight squeeze) up to the viewing platform and enjoy the panorama over the harbour and old part of town (Ramblas) – not for the faint-hearted though!

La Mercè   (U/E4)
Baroque church of the former Hospitalers' monastery. Now the

residence of the Capitania General. *Carrer de la Mercè*

Llotja (U/E3-4)
Maritime trade exchange, built from 1358 to 1390. *Plaça del Palau*

Palau de la Generalitat (U/D3)
This palatial building, seat of the state government of Catalonia, was built in the 15th century; its Renaissance façade, a century later. *Plaça de Sant Jaume*

Palau Episcopal (U/D3)
Episcopal palace, dating from the 12th century, partly on the site of the Roman city wall. *Carrer del Bisbe*

Palau de la Virreina (U/D4)
Palatial residence built for the Marquis of Castellbell, Viceroy of Peru. *Rambla, 99*

Santa Anna (U/D3)
Twelfth-century Romanesque church with fine Gothic cloisters. *Carrer de Santa Anna*

Santa Maria del Mar (U/E3)
Church built in the Catalan Gothic style (1329–70). Superb stained-glass rose window depicting the crowning of the Virgin Mary. *Near the Plaça del Palau*

MUSEUMS

Barcelona is home to the most important museums in Spain, outside Madrid. Below is a list of the most significant collections here:

Fundació Joan Miró (U/C5)
Numerous Miró pictures dating from 1914 to 1978. *Parc de Montjuïc*

Museu Arqueològic (U/C5)
Iberian, Greek and Roman finds discovered in Barcelona. *Parc de Montjuïc*

Museu d'Art de Catalunya (U/B5)
World's finest collection of Romanesque and Gothic mural paintings. *Palau Nacional de Montjuïc*

Museu Frederic Marès (U/D3)
Sculptures dating from Greek and Roman times down to the 18th century, housed in the medieval town residence of the Earl of Barcelona, later seat of the Spanish Inquisition. *Comtes de Barcelona, 10*

Museu d'Història de la Ciutat (U/D3)
Many exhibits illustrating the history of the city, including Roman relics found in Barcelona. *Veguer*

Museu Marítim (U/D4)
Begun in 1378, the former Royal Shipyard Drassanes – in which 30 galleys could be constructed simultaneously – now houses models and documents relating to Catalonia's seafaring tradition. *Plaça Portal de la Pau, 1*

Museu Picasso (U/E3)
More than 100 works from various creative periods of the great Spanish artist. *Carrer Montcada, 15*

PARKS & SQUARES

Montjuïc (U/B-D5-6)
⋙ The 173-m-high Montjuïc achieved world fame in 1992 when the Olympic Games were staged in Barcelona – it is the site of the Olympic Stadium. The 17th-century fortress at its summit served as a prison until after the Spanish Ci-

vil War. Today, the moat is a training ground for the city's archers. Magnificent view over the city and the sea from the fortress, which can be reached by cable car. Below the fortress is an amusement park.

Parc de la Ciutadella (U/E3)
Very beautiful park on the opposite side of the city to Montjuïc. This was once the site of a huge fortress, built by Philip V in the 18th century to keep in check the unruly Catalans. It was demolished between 1869 and 1888. On the grounds is a man-made lake with its own flamingo colony. At the far end is the entrance to the zoo.

Plaça de Catalunya (U/D3)
❂ The heart of the city: loud, lively, crowded pavements, tooting car horns, exhaust fumes. Nevertheless, this is the place to see and be seen in the cafés, whether young or old, rich or poor. Handy traffic junction: underneath the square are Metro and high-speed railway stations. During festivals an open-air stage is erected on the lawn in the centre.

Plaça Reial (U/D4)
⚐ The most beautiful square in the Gothic Quarter, situated near the harbour-end of the Rambla. With its arcade cafés, against a backdrop of palms, fountains and Gaudí's Modernist street lamps, this is a favourite meeting place for young people and, before the Olympics, for drug dealers and their customers, too. From time to time, open-air rock concerts are held here.

Tibidabo (O)
❂ The locals also call this the magic mountain. Fabulous amusement park high over the city, in the northwest of Barcelona, in the foothills of the mountains. A favourite attraction for all age groups is the museum dedicated to gaming machines.

RESTAURANTS

Botafumeiro (U/B1)
Fine Galician fish and shellfish delicacies await you here. *Daily; Gran de Gràcia, 81; Tel. 932 18 42 30; category 2*

Can Culleretes (U/D4)
Traditional restaurant, serving good old-fashioned Catalan food. *Closed Sun evenings and Mon; Carrer Quintana 3; Tel. 933 17 64 85; category 2*

Casa Isidoro (U/C4)
Traditional cuisine, attracting many regular guests. Specialities include brains in black butter. For gourmets. *Daily, except Sun; Les Flors, 12; Tel. 934 41 11 39; category 2*

Neichel (O)
Finest restaurant in town. Excellent Catalan fish dishes. *Closed Sat lunchtime, Sun, August and Christmas; Av. Pedralbes, 16; Tel. 932 03 84 08; category 1*

Pa i Trago (U/C4)
A favourite spot amongst the locals for high-quality regional cuisine and cosy atmosphere. *Daily, except Mon; Parlament, 41; Tel. 934 41 13 20; category 2–3*

Set Portes (U/E4)
The "seven doors" has enjoyed a reputation with lovers of fine fish dishes since 1836. Generous helpings. *Daily; Passeig d'Isabell II, 14; Tel. 933 19 30 33; category 2*

HOTELS

Since the Olympic Games, Barcelona has been able to offer a wide range of guest accommodation. Prices are, however, on a par with other major cities.

Condes de Barcelona y
Anexo   (U/C2)
Stay in a wonderful Art Nouveau building on the Passeig de Gràcia. A favourite haunt of bullfighters. *183 rooms; Passeig de Gràcia, 75; Tel. 934 88 11 52; Fax 934 67 47 85; category 1*

Lleo   (U/C3)
Close to the university, this modest hotel is highly recommended. *81 rooms; Pelai, 22–24; Tel. 933 18 13 12; Fax 934 12 26 57; category 2*

Oriente   (U/D4)
Traditional hotel in the heart of town. Magnificent dining room. Orwell was a guest here. *142 rooms; Rambla, 45–47; Tel. 933 02 25 58; Fax 934 12 38 19; category 2*

Rivoli Rambla   (U/D3)
Designer hotel on the Rambla, close to the Plaça Catalunya. Art-Déco-style rooms. *87 rooms; Ramblas dels estudis, 128; Tel. 933 02 66 43; Fax 933 01 93 44; category 1*

SHOPPING

Whatever you're looking for, you're almost sure to find it in shopper's paradise Barcelona. Fashions, art, antiques, bric-a-brac, books, fine foods – all this and more on such shopping streets as the Passeig de Gràcia. Don't miss the city's amazing variety of markets; La Boqueria on the Rambla is the finest.

SPORTS & LEISURE

Thanks to its role as Olympic host in 1992, Barcelona boasts all kinds of sporting facilities. Water-sports enthusiasts in particular find endless opportunities. There's also golf, archery, horse riding and tennis, and in the mountains to the north of the city, skiing. If you prefer being a spectator, visit a bullfight or sample the atmosphere at the stadium of Barcelona FC. It is even possible to play pelota, a typical Basque ball game: *Principal Palacio, Plaça del Teatre, Rambla*

ENTERTAINMENT

Nick Havanna   (U/C2)
Barcelona's classic design bar. Plenty of action till three in the morning. *Carrer Roselló, 208*

La Paloma   (U/C4)
Pure nostalgia in Europe's most beautiful ballroom. Dancing begins at midnight. *Tigre, 27*

La Xampanyeria   (U/B–C 2)
Where the rich and the beautiful – and those who think they are – get together and drink Spanish sparkling wine to the "talk of the town". *Provença, 236*

INFORMATION

Turisme de Barcelona
Passeig de Gràcia, 107, Palau Robert; Tel. 932 38 40 00; Fax 932 38 40 00 (U/D4); *Railway station: Barcelona-Sants: Tel. 934 91 44 31* (U/A 4); *Airport: Tel. 934 78 05 65* (O); *www.barcelonaturisme.com.*

You'll find more information about Barcelona in the MARCO POLO guide *Barcelona*.

Fishing villages and artists' colonies

*Sit back and relax in picturesque bays
and cosy bars*

A narrow road winds its way through the foothills of the Pyrenees. And what lies alongside it? Nothing. To the left, the rocks crumble away in places, tumbling down over the edge of the cliffs to the foaming sea below. Ahead of you on the horizon, the shimmering blue of the sky blends into that of the sea and merges with distant granite rock formations. A few

*The Costa Brava's "white city":
Cadaqués*

dazzling specks of white give depth to the contours; fishing villages probably, beyond the mountains, embedded in enchanting countryside. Why look any further? The northern part of the Costa Brava seems strangely quiet at first. Hadn't we read somewhere about the hustle and bustle of places like Lloret and Platja d'Aro. And here? Certainly, on the narrow beaches of Portbou, Port de Selva or Port de Llançà tourists and locals lie side by side in the sun, but not like sardines in a tin,

---

Hotel and restaurant prices

Hotels

Category 1: more than £ 39
Category 2: £ 23 to £ 39
Category 3: less than £ 23

Prices are for two people sharing a double room, including a modest breakfast.

Restaurants

Category 1: more than £ 23
Category 2: £ 10 to £ 23
Category 3: less than £ 10

Prices include an hors d'œuvre, a main course, a dessert, and drinks for one person.

Important abbreviations

Av.	Avinguda (Avenue)	**Sta.**	Santa (Saint)
s/n	sin número (no number)	**Urb.**	Urbanización (holiday village)

---

as elsewhere. The nightlife has a rural feel to it and is nothing at all like the blaring disco atmosphere of the boulevards down south. Thank goodness. A few fishermen sit in front of a small bar, drinking aniseed brandy, a dog blinks into the setting sun, teenagers rattle past on their mopeds. If this sounds like your idea of a relaxing holiday, then this is the place for you. The fish on the menu is freshly caught and the prices are reasonable too. Welcome to the Costa Brava.

CADAQUÉS

(101/F4) ★ Approaching Cadaqués from the direction of El Port de la Selva, having followed the course of the zig-zag road from the mountains to the sea, you might be forgiven for thinking you're on a Hollywood set. A small, completely white town of 1,500 inhab-

itants nestles in the bay, whose water is an unbelievable shade of blue. Not a high-rise block in sight. The tallest structure is the tower of the Baroque parish church. People say this is the most beautiful place on the Costa Brava – and who are we to disagree?

Like all other towns along the coast, the fishing village fell victim to countless pirate raids. The worst of these was at the hands of a certain Khayr ad-Din Barbarossa, who laid waste to Cadaqués in 1543 and even set fire to the church. Subsequently, the villagers became more vigilant and gained a reputation for invincibility and extreme self-assurance.

Cadaqués became famous on account of its important artists' colony. Painters, writers, musicians were drawn to the "most beautiful village in the world": Pablo Picasso, Marcel Duchamp, Henri Matisse, Max Ernst, Paul Eluard,

---

MARCO POLO SELECTION: NORTH COAST

1 Bay of Port de la Selva
Like a blue lagoon, ringed with a string of white pearl fishing boats (page 42)

2 Cadaqués
If you've not seen Cadaqués, its museums and bars, you haven't seen the Costa Brava (page 36)

3 La Galiota
Pure, unadulterated enjoyment! One of the most original restaurants on the Costa Brava (page 38)

4 Museo Perrot Moore
Famous private collection, with works by artists ranging from Brueghel to Dalí (page 37)

5 Port Lligat
Unspoilt fishing village. Interesting oddity: Salvador Dalí's house (page 41)

6 Sant Pere de Rodes
The most impressive ruin on the Costa Brava. The view is unparalleled (page 43)

Federico García Lorca, André Breton, Gabriel García Márquez – and of course Salvador Dalí. His father was born here, and Dalí himself spent the summer holidays of his childhood on his parents' estate. Later, Dalí moved with his wife Gala and their entourage to nearby Port Lligat. Thanks to him, Cadaqués has retained its unspoilt charm. During the tourism and construction boom, the fishermen of Cadaqués saw a chance to jump on the bandwagon and make their fortune by building hotels to attract more tourists. Dalí, however, did everything in his power to prevent the rapid urbanization of the village at the expense of its good looks and character. Today, people are grateful and the tourists are still coming thick and fast. Don't bother trying to drive to the centre of the village – there are too few parking spaces. There are car parking facilities on the outskirts, from where it is just a five-minute walk to the beach or to the Rambla. Be sure to wear sturdy, flat shoes, since the medieval cobblestones are less than kind to your ankles!

SIGHTS

Castell de les Creus
Also known as Sant Jaume, an old, ruined fortress on a hill overlooking the town. Some parts of the old town fortifications can still be seen.

Iglesia Parroquial
The old parish church of Santa Maria was destroyed in 1543 by pirates. The Baroque building that replaced it dates from the end of the 16th century. The most valuable item inside the church is the Baroque altar, carved by Pau Costa in 1727. *Town centre*

Picasso House
Situated on the beach, adjacent to the Casa Serinyena, the tall, white house with blue window frames. Unfortunately, visitors are not allowed to enter the house, but a plaque commemorates the artist who lived here in 1910.

MUSEUMS

Museo Municipal de Arte Contemporáneo
Works by Dalí and Picasso and other artists who were in some way linked with Cadaqués. *Easter–end-Sept, Mon–Sat 10.30 am–1 pm and 5 pm–9 pm, Sun 11 am–1 pm; Carrer de Narcís Monturiol, 15; admission: 300 ptas*

Museo Perrot Moore
★ One of the most important private art collections in Europe, covering works from the 15th to the 20th century, by such artists as Braque, Gris, Brueghel, Van Dyck, Rubens, Toulouse-Lautrec, Matisse, Miró and Dalí. *June–Sept, daily 5 pm–9 pm, guided tours at 5 pm and 6.30 pm; Carrer Unió/Riera de Sant Vicente; admission: 300 ptas*

RESTAURANTS

Can Josep
Modest restaurant serving fish dishes. *Carrer de Sant Antoni; no Tel.; category 3*

Casa Anita
High-quality, reasonably priced home cooking. *Carrer Miquel Rosset, 16; Tel. 972 25 84 71; category 3*

Casa Pelayo
Here you'll find various fish specialities, such as *suquet de peix*

(monkfish with potatoes). *Pruna 11; Tel. 972 25 83 53; category 2*

Don Quijote
Reputable address with pleasant terrace. For lovers of meat and fish. *Daily, except Mon and Nov; Av. Caridad Seriñana, 5; Tel. 972 25 81 41; category 2*

Es Baluard
A stylish restaurant set amidst ancient fortifications. Fine fish dishes. *Daily, except Thurs and Oct–May; Riba Nemesio Llorens, 2; Tel. 972 25 81 83; category 2*

La Galiota
★ Quite simply the best restaurant in Cadaqués. This unpretentious establishment on the first floor of the house is only a five-minute walk from the promenade. Here, Nuri and Pepita Rivera await you with a range of meat and fish specialities from the Empurdá region, including *botifarras dulces* (sweet sausages), *lubina a la Galiota* (sea perch à la maison), *soufflé al Grand Marnier* (soufflé with orange liqueur). *Daily 2 pm–4 pm and 9 pm–11 pm, closed Oct–14 June; Narcís Monturiol, 9; Tel. 972 25 81 87; category 2*

SHOPPING

Not surprisingly, Cadaqués's reputation as an artists' mecca is reflected in its commercial activities. It is home to numerous art shops and galleries. The galleries listed here carry works from the 20th century.

Domus Arte y Antigüedades y Decoración
Art dealership, ceramics, textiles, wall hangings. *Carrer Unió, 1, behind the Perrot Moore Museum*

Galería Cadaqués
Horta d'en Sanés, 7

Galería Carlos Losano
Carrer Font Vellas, s/n

Galería d'Art E. Fernandez
Carrer Unió, s/n

Libreria Passeig Marítim
Books focusing on the village and its artists, such as Dalí and Picasso. You can also buy newspapers and magazines here. *Passeig del Mar, 6*

Taller Galería Fort
Horta d'en Sanés, 9

Tropico
Wonderful artificial fruit carved out of wood and painted, also masks in all shapes and sizes. *Carrer Santa Margarita*

Weekly market
Vegetables, wine, fish, seafood – every *Mon 8 am–1 pm*. A feast for all the senses. *Riera, close to the large car parks*

HOTELS

Hotel Blaumar
Well-tended estate with garden and swimming pool, 27 rooms with air conditioning. *Massa d'Or 21; Tel. 972 15 90 20; Fax 972 15 93 36; category 2*

Cala D'Or
Modest hotel with a small restaurant. *18 rooms; Carrer Tortola, s/n; Tel. 972 25 81 49; category 3*

Hostal S'Aguarda
Reasonably priced hotel. *27 rooms; closed Nov; Carretera Port Lli-*

gat, 28; Tel. 972 25 80 82; Fax 972 25 10 57; category 2

Playa Sol

The best hotel in the village has a swimming pool and affords a breathtaking view over the bay of Cadaqués. *49 rooms; closed 20 Dec–end of Feb; Platja Pianc, 5; Tel. 972 25 81 00; Fax 972 25 80 54; category 1*

Hotel Port Lligat

This attractive hotel is situated just a few kilometres from Cadaqués in Port Lligat. Several of the rooms with a terrace boast a fine view over the bay and Dalí's house. The swimming pool has a 10-m diving tower. There is a small beach just below the grounds. *30 rooms; closed in winter; Port Lligat, s/n; Tel. 972 25 81 62; Fax 972 25 86 43; category 1*

Ubaldo

This unpretentious hotel lies near the centre of the village. *26 rooms; Carrer Unió, s/n; Tel. 972 25 81 25; category 2*

SPORTS & LEISURE

Although Cadaqués's beaches cannot be ranked amongst the most beautiful on the coast – they are too stony for that – they do offer a wide range of water sports. Portdoguer, Es Portal, Portitxó, Es Poal and Es Pianc are the most notable.

Water sports

Club de Vela, *Platja Gran; no Tel.; summer only*

Escola Nàutica Cap de Creus, on the beach at *Port Lligat; no Tel.; summer only*

On Saturdays, in summer, Sardana – a typical Catalan folk dance – is performed in the Passeig. Feel free to join in if you wish. You'll be more than welcome.

ENTERTAINMENT

Café Galeón

Anybody who is anybody comes here in the evenings! The guests come from all over the world – and they all bring their dogs with them! *Plaza, 15 (Passeig)*

Casino de Cadaqués

Meeting place for the artistically inclined and popular with the locals, too. The casino boasts its own library and also holds exhibitions. *Plaça Dr. Tremols, 1; Tel. 972 25 82 68*

Es Porró

Disco and bar with live music in the summer. Things start heating up around 1 am. *Portal de la Font*

Espoal

This pretty little bar lies at the end of the bay. A good place to wind up a day trip or to head for on a constitutional after your evening meal! *Carrer d'es Pianc, 3*

La Habana

The cosiest bar in Cadaqués, where the owner himself is known to take up his guitar and perform a few songs for his guests. *Punta d'en Pampa*

L'Hostal

One of the best jazz clubs in Spain. Mick Jagger and Gabriel García Márquez have both sampled the atmosphere here. Dalí designed the bar logo. *Passeig, 8*

Passeig

◈ ✤ If it's excitement you're after, then this is the place to come. Accomplished – and aspiring – masters of the art of living meet here, especially in the evenings, when Cadaqués really comes to life. A whiff of hashish laces the air.

La Xixonenca

◈ Cadaqués's top ice-cream parlour. Speciality: *horchata de chufa* – almond milk. *Carrer Vigilant, s/n, next to the tourist information office*

INFORMATION

Oficina Municipal de Turisme

Daily, except Sun, 10 am–1 pm and 5 pm–8 pm; Carrer Cotxe, 2; Tel. 972 25 83 15; Fax 972 15 94 42

SURROUNDING AREA

Cala Nans   (101/F4-5)

Nature-lovers should not miss the 90-minute walk along the coast to the south; it's well worth the effort. The path takes you from Sa Conca as far as the promontory at Cala Nans with its lighthouse. Off the coast lie the Cucurucuc de les Seves islands: pretty view.

Cap de Creus   (101/F4)

◁▷ Picturesque bays flank the Cap de Creus headland to the north of Cadaqués, which can be reached along a coastal footpath. The round trip takes about three hours. A lighthouse stands on this most easterly point of Spain and the Club Méditerranée has set up a holiday complex in one of the bays.

El Pení   (101/E4)

◁▷ A must for photographers and those who would like to sample the breathtaking view of Cadaqués, its bays, the mountains and – weather permitting – the entire north coast, is the climb up the 605-m-high El Pení to the southwest of

Boats on the beach at Port Lligat, below Dalí's house

Cadaqués. The two-hour hike (round trip) takes you past the old Ermita de Sant Sebastià.

Port Lligat   (101/F4)

★ This small, very beautiful fishing village lies in a bay just a 30-minute-walk away from Cadaqués. It was here that Salvador Dalí lived and worked, together with his wife Gala, in their eye-catching house, which was originally a group of small fishermen's cottages, which they "cobbled" together. Dalí held Port Lligat to be one of the most beautiful places in the world, but on the death of his wife, he wrote that it had become one of the most desolate. He left to go and live in Púbol, where Gala lies buried. Following Dalí's death, the villagers of Port Lligat wanted to turn his unique house into a museum. Finally, now that the dispute amongst the heirs has been settled, both houses have been opened to the public. The cost of renovation totalled some 1 million pounds. *15 March–6 Jan: Tues–Sun, 10.30 am–6 pm; 15 June–15 Sept: daily until 9 pm; guided tours only; admission: 1,300 ptas*

LLANÇÀ

(101/D3) This is, if you like, the first tourist colony on the northern Costa Brava. The contrast to the concrete jungle further south couldn't be more marked, however. The down-to-earth character of the people in this rural area has prevented the ruthless plastering-over of the charms of this small town of 3,000 inhabitants. So you'll still be able to find idyllic corners and streets lined with whitewashed houses and tiny bars. The fishing village attracts many visitors in the summer, mainly from Figueres and nearby France. Fishing village? Llançà lies inland, approximately one kilometre from the coast! The explanation is simple: marauding pirates once drove the inhabitants to take refuge in their more protected village of Llançà-Vila. Later, the harbour played an important role in the export of wine and olives to Italy and France. Marble was also quarried nearby, which brought the village a degree of prosperity even before the onset of tourism.

SIGHTS

Iglesia Parroquial de San Vincente

Eighteenth-century Baroque church on the *Plaça Major.*

Torre de Defensa

Fifteenth-century fortified tower built to ward off pirates. In the centre of the village on the *Plaça Major.*

RESTAURANTS

La Brasa

Catalan restaurant with pretty terrace. *Closed from Dec–Feb; Plaça Catalunya, 6; Tel. 972 38 02 02; category 2*

Can Manuel

Family-run restaurant with fine fish dishes. Try the chef's own *gambas* recipe! *Daily, except Sun evenings; Plaça del Port, 9; Tel. 972 38 01 12; category 2*

Can Narra

Modest, but fresh and lovingly prepared fish dishes. *Daily, except*

Sun evenings; Carrer de Castellà, 5; Tel. 972 38 01 78; category 3

El Racó del Port

This fish restaurant is situated on the harbour. *Daily, except Mon. Closed 1 Oct–31 March; Plaça del Port, 3; Tel. 972 38 00 80; category 2*

La Vela

Good fish restaurant, no frills. *Closed Wed and 15 Oct–15 Nov; Pintor Martínez Lozano, 3; Tel. 972 38 04 75; category 2*

Locally produced olive oil and wine can be purchased in the shops in Llançà; ceramics too.

Beri

Pleasant hotel with swimming pool. *60 rooms; La Creu, 26; Tel. 972 38 01 98; Fax 972 12 13 12; category 3*

Berna

Agreeable hotel on the harbour, offering a pleasant view. *38 rooms; closed Oct–May (except Easter); Passeig Marítim, 13 (harbour); Tel. 972 38 01 50; Fax 972 12 15 09; category 2*

Carbonell

Modest accommodation. *33 rooms; closed 26 Sept–Easter; Major, 19; Tel. 972 38 02 09; Fax 972 38 02 09; category 3*

La Goleta

Small, modest but pleasant hotel. *38 rooms; Pintor Tarruella, 12; Tel. 972 38 01 25; Fax 972 12 06 86; category 2*

Gri-Mar

Attractive hotel with swimming pool. *45 rooms; closed 1 Oct–Easter; Carretera de Portbou; Tel. 972 38 01 67; Fax 972 38 12 00; category 2*

Tennis

Tenis Club Grifeu, Tenis Club San Genis. Both *Carretera Portbou; no Tel.*

Water sports

Club Nàutic Llançà; *Tel. 972 38 07 10*; windsurfing, boards for rent; *Platja del Cau; no Tel.*

Patronat Municipal de Turisme

Av. d'Europa, 37; Tel. 972 38 08 55; Fax 972 38 12 58

El Port de la Selva   (101/E3)

This small but equally idyllic fishing village, with its 1,000 inhabitants, lies some 8 km southeast of Llançà. It is set in a fabulous ★ bay, whose waters are as calm as any lake, and the mountains of the Sierra de Montaña Negra, also known as the Sierra de Roda, provide a stunning backdrop. The mountains must have been covered by dense forests at one time, since the word "selva" means "jungle". Together they formed an impenetrable barrier, which meant that it was only possible to reach the village by boat. In prehistoric times, this fact afforded the inhabitants a degree of safety. Indeed artefacts testify to an Iron

The ruined monastery Sant Pere de Rodes, once the seat of the Benedictines

Age settlement: stone knives, ceramics and, near *Punta del Pi*, a burial site with 70 graves.

Sant Pere de Rodes (101/D4)

★ ✴ The most important monastery ruins on the Costa Brava stand in the hills above Port de la Selva. A narrow, winding road leads up towards the complex. The last part, however, must be negotiated on foot. It's worth the effort. The impressive Benedictine abbey was first mentioned in AD 879, although some historians maintain it was built on older ruins, namely those of an ancient temple of Venus. The Romanesque monastery church was consecrated in 1022. Completion of the structure, with its three naves, was quite an achievement, considering the rough terrain surrounding the site. In the 11th and 12th centuries, the monastery flourished, attracting many rich pilgrims. The monks were able to acquire land in the area and other treasures, including a famous library. The prosperity of the monastery undoubtedly had a beneficial effect on the villages around it, in the form of an exchange of goods and services.

From 1300 onwards, though, ever more frequent raids and thefts, countered by ultimately fruitless additions to the fortifications, signalled the gradual decline of the monastery. Pilgrims stayed away and the increasingly impoverished monks were eventually forced to leave around the time of the French Revolution.

The monastery is currently being renovated, and is certainly worth a visit. This in spite of the fact that much of the decorative details on the various buildings have been destroyed over the centuries and that the most prized treasure of Sant Pere de Rodes, a valuable Romanesque Bible, is now to be found in the Bibliothèque Nationale in Paris. *Daily 9 am–2 pm and 4 pm–8 pm; in winter 10.30 am–1 pm and 3 pm–6 pm*

Castell Sant Salvador (101/D4)

◁▷ On a mountain summit above the monastery of Sant Pere de Rodes stands the ruined castle Sant Salvador. From here, you have a truly breathtaking view over the bays, the sea, the monastery and the Pyrenees to the west. All in all, it's probably the most stunning panorama along the entire Costa Brava. This could go some way to explaining the medieval legend that the Holy Grail, the drinking goblet used by Christ at the Last Supper, was once kept under guard here.

PORTBOU

(101/D2) This is the first town you come to after crossing the border from France. Portbou lies between the mountains and a deep bay and has some 2,400 inhabitants. Its beach is very pretty, but unfortunately quite narrow and stony. The town itself boasts an attractive Rambla with small bars and restaurants. Portbou is a favourite destination for French day-trippers in particular, since they can eat out relatively cheaply here. The Festa Major in July lasts several days and attracts visitors from far and near: this is when the otherwise quiet little town really lets loose!

A common grave in the cemetery is the last resting place of German writer and philosopher Walter Benjamin. On the run from the Nazis, he took his own life in Portbou on 27 September 1940.

SIGHTS

Railway station

◁▷ It may sound strange, but the railway station at Portbou, high up in a commanding position over the town, is in fact its greatest attraction. This is due, firstly, to its location, perched upon the Roca Foradada and, secondly, to its status as a major junction on the line between Paris and Barcelona. Nothing special about that, you might think, but a quirk of fate compels all passengers to alight here and get onto different trains, as is the case at Russian-Polish stations. Spain's railways operate on tracks with a different gauge to the rest of continental Europe, namely the Russian one. Only luxury trains, such as the "Talgo" are able to adjust gauges automatically.

RESTAURANTS

All along the promenade you'll find little restaurants, mainly specializing in fish – which of course couldn't be fresher!

L'Áncora

Small restaurant serving a variety of fish and other seafood delicacies. *Daily, except Mon evenings and Tues, closed Nov–3 Dec; Passeig de la Sardana; Tel. 972 39 00 25; category 3*

HOTELS

In addition to the two hotels named below, Portbou offers a range of accommodation in small hotels and modest B&Bs.

Comodoro
Modest hotel with a small, reasonably priced restaurant. *15 rooms; open 1 June–15 Oct; Méndez Núñez, 1; Tel. 972 39 01 87; category 3*

La Masia
Pretty little hotel (no restaurant) close to the beach and harbour. *14 rooms; Passeig de la Sardana, 1; Tel. 972 39 03 72; Fax 972 12 50 66; category 2*

SPORTS & LEISURE

In the bay *Cala Petita* you can swim, surf or take a romantic boat trip. Diving is also possible in the other bays around Portbou.

ENTERTAINMENT

Portbou cannot offer a spectacular nightlife, but several of the small cafés and bars on the Rambla and along the promenade are open late into the evening in the summer months.

INFORMATION

Oficina d'Informació
Passeig Lluís Companys; Tel. 972 12 51 61; Fax 972 12 51 23

SURROUNDING AREA

Colera (101/D2)
Picturesque fishing village (pop. 450) with a long, pebble beach. Colera lies in a valley that cuts into the coastline and is spanned by a mighty railway bridge. In the evening, you can enjoy the unaffected atmosphere of village life; while sitting on the main square, in the shade of a huge plane tree, outside a café, taking in an *aperitivo* and a few *tapas*. The village's proper name is San Miguel de Colera, named after the tenth-century Romanesque monastery, whose ruins can still be visited on the Puig d'Esquers (603 m) nearby. This tourist backwater boasts three old cannons dating from 1789, which stand with their barrels pointing out to sea.

Colera can also claim extremely clear water, which is of particular interest to divers. The *Hostal Garbet (open April–Oct; Platja de Garbet, s/n; Tel. 972 38 90 02; category 3)* is a small hotel on the beach, which serves only breakfast. Close by there are several modest inns offering lunch. More information at the *Centre d'Iniciatives Turistiques Laboum, 34; Tel. 972 38 90 50; Fax 972 38 92 83*

La Jonquera (100/A2)
Border crossing into France to the west of Portbou (via the N 260 and the highway). Very beautiful 15th-century church with Romanesque portal.

Starting from La Jonquera, a trip to the mountain village of *Cantallops* (9 km west of La Jonquera) is recommended. From there on to the medieval castle *Castillo de Requesens.* The ruins of the ninth-century church Santa Maria de Requesens are well worth a visit.

Historical landscape by the sea

Both Greeks and Romans left their mark on the Riu Fluvià delta

As you travel south, you leave behind the purely picture-postcard beauty of the Costa Brava and encounter more variety in the landscape. You come across not only mountains, villages, bays and the sea, but also river estuaries, the largest area of marshland in Spain, a wine-growing plain and vegetable plantations. Following Dalí's tracks, you reach Figueres, try your luck in a castle-cum-casino or marvel at a 2,500-year-old mosaic floor. Between Doric columns, you catch a glimpse of the same sea across which the Greeks came so many centuries ago. The vivid green pine trees still sway in the sea breeze and an Attic god stands, captivated, his gaze directed far out across the Gulf of Roses. Hooked again.

L'ESCALA

(105/E2) Just another of those fishing villages? On closer inspection you'll find that this little town,

with its 4,700 inhabitants, may not have completely surrendered to the commercial demands of tourism, but it certainly has taken a large step in that direction. As you'd expect, the promenade along the main beach is lined with big hotel blocks, shops and bars – with the corresponding degree of hustle and bustle during the summer. In contrast, the area around the harbour, known as *norte*, is quieter, with small bars and cosy restaurants. L'Escala is the home port of some 50 small trawlers and, alongside Roses, is the most important fishing port on the Costa Brava. The richness in fish of the Gulf of Roses has drawn people to the area for centuries. The water quality is said to be excellent, even today. On the beach, the fishermen mend their nets – an idyllic image vis-à-vis the signs of a striving holiday industry, which, it is hoped, will not do as much damage both physically and psychologically as it did 20 years ago. What draws visitors to L'Escala today is its glorious past: the nearby ruined city of Empúries.

Medieval bridge with watchtower, in Besalú

Cementiri Vell
Neoclassical seaman's graveyard by the sea.

Monument a la Gent del Mar
Memorial to fishermen and seafarers on the La Punta promontory.

Sant Pere de l'Escala
Parish church with Renaissance façade (1761), in the centre of town. In the interior is a portrait of St Maxima, the female patron saint of L'Escala, and also a precious statue of St Peter.

RESTAURANTS

L'Escala has established for itself the reputation of being one of the best places on the Costa Brava to eat seafood. Be sure to treat yourself to a meal at one of its numerous restaurants.

Café Navili
Good old-fashioned fish restaurant at the harbour. *Daily, except Mon; Romeú de Corbera; Tel. 972 77 12 01; category 2*

Club Nàutic L'Escala
Reasonably priced meals and drinks. *La Clota, at the fishing port; Tel. 972 77 00 16; category 3*

Els Pescadors
Speciality: fish stew with potatoes and garlic. Don't miss it. *Daily, except Sun evenings, closed Nov; Port d'en Perris, 3; Tel. 972 77 07 28; category 2*

El Roser 2
Excellent fish restaurant. *Daily, except Wed, closed Feb; Passeig Lluís Albert, 1; Tel. 972 77 11 02; category 1*

Miryam
Restaurant with guest rooms. Excellent cuisine. *Closed beginning*

MARCO POLO SELECTION: GULF OF ROSES

1 A walk through Besalú
An imposing bridge takes you across the Riu Fluvià, straight into the Middle Ages. On the banks below, the old men sit fishing, as their forefathers did 800 years ago (page 54)

2 Teatro Museo Dalí
You don't have to be an expert to be fascinated by Salvador Dalí's Surrealist circus (page 53)

3 Ruins of Empúries
Fascinating Graeco-Roman settlement to the north of L'Escala (page 49)

4 Hacienda El Bulli
A three-star paradise for those wishing to experience something special (page 57)

5 Fish market in Roses
A feast for all the senses. Here, the richesbof the sea change hands. Picture-postcard Mediterranean setting (page 58)

6 Marshes of Empordà
Home to countless waterfowl; a corner of unspoilt countryside. A must for nature-lovers (page 59)

of Dec–mid-Jan; Rondo del Padró, 4; Tel. 972 77 02 87; category 1

SHOPPING

Boat owners can stock up on supplies at a number of specialist shops. Make a point of visiting the daily fish market at the port; from 8 am, you can watch the freshly landed catch of *sardinas* (sardines) being sold. The normal fish market opens at 3 pm.

HOTELS

Nieves Mar
The best hotel in town, situated by the sea, with a lovely view of the gulf. It also boasts the best fish restaurant in L'Escala. *75 rooms; closed Nov–March; Passeig Marítim, 8; Tel. 972 77 03 00; Fax 972 77 36 05; category 1*

El Roser
Reasonable hotel. Its restaurant can be recommended, too. *25 rooms; restaurant closed Mon; Iglesia, 7; Tel. 972 77 02 19; Fax 972 77 45 29; category 3*

Voramar
Mid-range hotel with pool. *36 rooms; Passeig Lluís Albert, 2; Tel. 972 77 01 08; Fax 972 77 03 77; category 2*

ENTERTAINMENT

The newer part of town *(sur)* offers a number of discos, which don't need to be listed separately. In the town centre *(norte)*, you'll find many small bars, which are open until late at night in the summer months. Don't miss the Sardana dancing on the *platja* every Wednesday in summer, from 10 pm.

SPORTS & LEISURE

L'Escala offers many opportunities to pursue all kinds of water sport. There is a beach close to the fishing boat moorings. To the south, the beaches at Platja de Riells or Cala Montgó, to the north, the wide, sandy Platja d'Empúries.

Water sports
Club Nàutic L'Escala, *La Clota, Puerto Perquero; Tel. 972 77 00 16; sailing courses in July and August*

Miniature golf
Avinguda Montgó; Tel. 972 77 07 48

Horse riding
Rancho Bruno, *Hipica Montgó; no Tel.*

Tennis
At the Nieves Mar hotel

INFORMATION

Oficina de Turisme
Plaça Escoles Nacionals, 1; Tel. 972 77 06 03; Fax 972 77 33 85

SURROUNDING AREA

Empúries   (105/E2)
★ Probably the largest Greco-Roman settlement in Spain is situated just 2 km north of L'Escala. Close to the sea is an area roughly the size of a small city, which is dotted with foundations and columns! And what's more, excavation work is not yet complete. For those interested in archaeology, this is undoubtedly the high point of any Costa Brava holiday.

About 580 BC the first Greek settlers made their way here

Site of Greco-Roman settlement at Empúries

from Phocaea in Asia Minor and created a harbour for trading purposes on the small island off the coast, calling it Emporion, which means trading centre. The harbour has long since silted up. Roughly 100 years later a new wave of Greek settlers arrived. They built a new settlement, Neopolis ("new town"), on the mainland opposite the old one, Palaiopolis ("old town"), and with it a new harbour. This became the largest and most important Greek colony in the western Mediterranean. The people of Palaiopolis (now part of the mainland) moved over to the new town, from where their economic and cultural influence – currency and alphabet – spread.

The indigenous Iberians also built a settlement here, called Indica, probably in the fourth century BC, incorporating the architectural and trading practices of their culturally superior predecessors. In 218 BC a Roman expeditionary force under the command of Scipio landed here, intending to make the existing settlement a mighty bridgehead against the Carthaginian forces who had already gained a foothold in mainland Spain. Later, Cato the Elder was sent in a final attempt to subdue the local inhabitants. Hannibal's brother Hasdrubal was the next to attack Empuriae, as it was now called, but suffered a crushing defeat. A period of incomparable prosperity began.

The Romans began building, not as conquerors, but as equal claimants to the territory. They constructed a new, larger town –

the largest Roman settlement on Spanish soil – which partly overlapped the existing Greek Neopolis. It consisted of massive fortified walls, temples, magnificent villas, market places, roads, palaces and even an arena and amphitheatre. Today, we can only speculate as to the size of the entire site, since excavation work is still under way.

Later, Julius Caesar had a colony for Roman war veterans built on the remains of the old Iberian settlement. Emporiae flourished, until c. AD 400, when the Visigoths arrived, conquered the city and declared it a bishopric. They built what was probably the first church on Spanish soil. Finally the city fell to the invading Normans, who laid waste to this cultural gem. In the centuries that followed, Empúries effectively ceased to exist, its ruined buildings plundered by the inhabitants of the surrounding towns and villages for construction materials. It was not until 1909 that the first tentative excavation work began, which is certain to unearth a few surprises in the years to come. One sensational find was the larger-than-life statue of the Greek god of healing, Asclepius, a copy of which stands in the museum on the site (the original is in the archaeological museum in Barcelona). As part of the preparations for the Olympic Games in 1992, a section of the ancient harbour was reconstructed to receive the Olympic torch on its way from Greece to Barcelona – you can't get more symbolic than that!

Allow yourself at least an afternoon (2–3 hours) to explore; only this way can you gain a real impression of the architecture and art of the entire site. Plan, also, to visit the Archaeological Museum, which is situated among the ruins. Its exhibits – some 2,500 years old – include ceramics, jewellery, weapons, household items, mosaics and statues. We recommend purchasing the guidebook (available in several European languages). *Daily, except Mon; 10 am–2 pm and 5 pm–7 pm; admission: 700 ptas*

Sant Marti d'Empúries   (105/D1–2)

This tiny village of only 100 souls is the immediate successor to the Greek settlement Palaiopolis, which was located on a small island. The dividing channel silted up and the island became part of the mainland. Sant Marti d'Empúries, too, has a certain historical significance; Charlemagne is said to have established the capital of the Carolingian county Empurda here in AD 812. The old church of Sant Marti was first mentioned in 843, destroyed by the Normans in 926 and rebuilt in 1248. Its renewed destruction in 1468 led to the building of the current structure between 1507 and 1538.

Sant Miquel de Fluvià   (104/C1)

The Romanesque parish church of this village on the Riu Fluvià dates from the 11th century, and is all that remains of an old Benedictine monastery.

Sant Pere Pescador   (105/D1)

If you're looking for a quiet, relaxing place to spend a holiday, look no further: this small fishing village with approximately 1,000 inhabitants, lies 3 km inland, on the banks of the Riu Fluvià. In the past, its secluded position hid it from pirates; today, it protects it against the hordes of tourists. The beach is fantastic: a seemingly endless expanse of fine sand, no massive hotel blocks, just a few holidaymakers on the camp sites off the beach. Take a look at the *Castillo*, the ruined walls of an old fortress, the *Iglesia Parroquial*, a 17th-century Baroque parish church, and the lagoon *Les Llaunes* in the estuary of the Riu Fluvià. Here, on both sides of the river, you'll find a wide variety of flora and fauna – an ideal spot for a relaxing walk.

Information: Ajuntament Sant Pere Pescador, Verge del Portalet, 10; Tel. 972 52 00 50

FIGUERES

(**100/B5**) For Costa Brava visitors, Figueres is an ideal choice for a day trip, and not just on a rainy day. The capital of the Empordà (pop. 35,000) can call a world-famous museum its own – more about that later. The town itself is not especially attractive, but nevertheless has several interesting sights. A stroll down the pretty Rambla with its many street cafés is also recommended.

Figueres has seen an eventful history. In the 12th century it fell to the Count of Barcelona and was granted its city charter by the Catalan King Jaime I in 1267. Shortly after this, Figueres was destroyed for the first time, at the hands of Count Hugo of Empúries and his army.

Not until 1743 was work begun on the construction of a fortress. It was to become the

"Surrealist temple": the Dalí Museum in Figueres

second biggest in Europe. On 11 May 1904, the town's most famous son was born here: Salvador Dalí. The town owes its fame and fortune largely to him to this day.

SIGHTS

Castell de Sant Ferran
The fortress was enclosed by an almost 5-km-long wall. Inside, 10,000 men with 5,000 horses were stationed. The interior of the fort is not open to the public. *On a hill, to the north-west of the town centre*

Iglesia Sant Pere
Fourteenth-century Gothic church situated in the centre of the old town. *Sant Pere s/n*

Statue of Narciso Monturiol
The monument stands on the main square on the Rambla. Monturiol was a Catalan inventor (1819–95). His most famous achievement was the building of

a wooden underwater craft, "Ictineo", which put into the harbour at Barcelona in 1861.

MUSEUMS

Museo del Empurdán

Important collection of regional artefacts, including Greek and Roman finds. There are also documents relating to the history of the town and numerous works by Picasso, Miró and of course Dalí. *Rambla; Tues–Sun, 11 am–1 pm and 3.30 pm–7 pm (July–Sept); 11.30 am–5.15 pm (Oct–June)*

Teatro Museo Dalí

★ This exhibition on its own is reason enough to come to Figueres. And that is what several hundred thousand visitors do each year. The majority are artistic laymen, who then emerge from the building as if from a circus big top, amused and enthralled by the eccentric and bizarre visual world of the Surrealist master. The museum is housed in the former *Teatro Municipal (Municipal Theatre)*. Dalí first exhibited works here at the tender age of 14. The theatre was destroyed during the Spanish Civil War and was reopened as a museum in 1974 – crowned by a mighty dome. A most fantastic – in the true sense of the word – collection of the fruits of the maestro's imagination. *July–Sept, daily 9 am–7.45 pm; Oct–June, Tues–Sun 10.30 am–5.15 pm; admission tickets also valid for the Museo del Empurdán; Sant Pere, s/n; Tel. 972 50 56 97; admission: 1,000 ptas*

RESTAURANTS

Can Jeroni

A traditional-style restaurant, serving excellent Catalan cuisine. *Lunchtime only, closed Sun; Carrer Castelló, 36; Tel. 972 50 09 83; category 2*

Empordà

Sample here the best Empordà cuisine has to offer, such as rabbit pâté with mint or pieces of turbot in apple vinegar. 15 guest rooms. *Antigua Carretera de Francia; 1.5 km north of Figueres; Tel. 972 50 05 62; category 1*

Duràn

❖ Very pleasant restaurant in the town centre, also offering guest rooms. The locals like to come here as well to indulge in the house speciality, *espalda de cordero a la ampurdanesa* (shoulder of mutton in the traditional, local style). Good fish, too. *Lasauca, 5; Tel. 972 50 12 50; category 2*

The grave of Salvador Dalí

Mystery surrounds the last resting place of Dalí. Originally, he wanted to be buried in his castle at Púbol, alongside Gala, his wife. On his deathbed he whispered his last wishes to the mayor of Figueres – and only to him. Dalí was buried then in his museum, under an unmarked stone slab in the floor. Without realizing it, countless visitors to the museum wander daily over his grave.

Mas Pau

Superb cuisine served up in a beautiful 17th-century villa, which lies outside Figueres. Crowned with a Michelin star, specialities are game and fish. The villa is also a very pleasant, quiet hotel with garden and swimming pool. Book early! *Closed in winter; 5 km west of Figueres, on the road to Olot; Avinyonet de Puigventós; Tel. 972 54 61 54; category 1*

Viarnés

❧Regional cooking, attractive dining room and many locals amongst the guests. *Closed Sun evenings and Mon, also first half of June and first half of Nov; Pujada del Castell, 23; Tel. 972 50 07 91; category 2*

SHOPPING

Art Surrealista

Posters, books, T-shirts – all with Dalí motifs. *Carrer Sant Pere*

Librería Surrealista

Everything for the Dalí fan – something for every pocket. *Gala i Salvador Dalí-Plaça (directly in front of the museum)*

HOTELS

Duràn

Luxury hotel. *65 rooms; Lasauca, 5; Tel. 972 50 12 50; Fax 972 50 26 09; category 2*

Los Ángeles

Modest establishment with 40 rooms, but no restaurant. *Barceloneta, 10; Tel. 972 51 06 61; Fax 972 51 07 00; category 3*

Pirineos

Hotel offering a medium standard of comfort with its own restaurant. *Closed Mon. 53 rooms; Ronda Barcelona, 1; Tel. 972 50 03 12; Fax 972 50 07 66; category 2*

Ronda

No frills hotel. *47 rooms; Ronda Barcelona, 104; Tel. 972 50 39 11; Fax 972 50 16 82; category 2–3*

Torremirona

Luxury hotel with park-like grounds, a swimming pool, its own golf course and a fine restaurant, approximately 10 km outside Figueres on the secondary road to Olot. *59 rooms; Navata; Tel. 972 56 67 00; Fax 972 65 67 67; category 1–2*

Travé

Hotel with swimming pool. *72 rooms; Carretera de Olot; Tel. 972 50 05 91; Fax 972 67 14 83; category 2*

INFORMATION

Oficina de Turisme

Plaça del Sol; Tel. 972 50 31 55; Fax 972 67 31 66

SURROUNDING AREA

Besalú   (103/D4)

★ A visit to Besalú means a journey into the early Middle Ages. The town of approximately 2,000 inhabitants lies 25 km southwest of Figueres. The outstanding feature of the town is undoubtedly the mighty, eight-arched bridge, which spans the Riu Fluvià and dates from the 11th century. Its two imposing watchtowers, together with parts of the old city wall, testify to the importance of Besalù; under the Romans it was a provincial centre, which was later overrun by the Visigoths. The Count of Besalù made the town

Fourteenth-century moated castle in Peralada

his seat in the ninth century. In the upper part of town, all that remains of the Monestir de Sant Pere is the church of the same name, with its ambulatory and bell tower, consecrated in AD 1000. The church of Sant Vicenc, a Romanesque building with three naves, also displays early Gothic features. Of the former chapel Santa Maria, adjacent to the Castell de Besalú (c. 1000), little is still visible, but it is worth taking a look at. In the eastern part of town is the old Jewish ritual bath *(Mikvah)*, also a relic of the Romanesque era. The synagogue has unfortunately not stood the test of time. To round off your stay, why not pause on the Plaça Major, a fine square lined with arcades. *Information: Oficina de Turisme, Plaça de la Libertat; Tel. 972 59 12 40*

El Far d'Empordà (100/B5)

A small village to the east of Figueres. On a hill stands a magnificent square-based Romanesque fortified church.

Peralada (100/B-C4)

A pretty little town of 1,300 souls, north of Figueres in the middle of a wine region. The white wine produced here is highly recommended and goes especially well with seafood – a good souvenir perhaps? In the town itself, take a look at the former monastery of *Sant Domènec* with its Romanesque cloisters from the 11th century. The main attraction in Peralada is, however, the *casino*, surely one of the most beautiful in the world. It is housed in the *castillo*, an impressive 14th-century castle surrounded by a flooded moat, its exterior dominated by its mighty walls and formidable round towers. Inside, in addition to the casino, you'll find an important art collection (including exhibits from Sant Pere de Rodes) and a fine library. Play baccarat, chemin de fer and roulette in truly exquisite surroundings. Blow your winnings (or drown your sorrows) in the stylish restaurant! *Castell de Peral-*

ada; high season, open until 5 am, otherwise until 4 am; Tel. 972 53 81 25

Vilabertrán   (100/B4)

This suburb of Figueres is the site of the noteworthy monastery Santa Maria de Vilabertrán, built in the Romanesque style. The three-apse church, the cloisters and bell tower date from the 11th century, the abbot's palace is a Gothic addition.

ROSES

(101/D–E5) It would be an exaggeration to maintain that Roses, with its 10,000 inhabitants, is still a jewel in the Costa Brava crown, for mass tourism has put paid to that. No sooner had they set eyes on the first broad beach in this northern part of the coast, than the building speculators stepped in. The wide curve of the bay is plastered with hotels and apartment blocks. Nevertheless, the beach remains beautiful and if you gaze out to sea, you can still enjoy one of those sensational sunrise or sunset spectacles for which Roses is prized. The fact that the promenade has been ruined so completely is all the more upsetting because Roses itself is set in such beautiful countryside. The bay is wide, while the Pyrenees provide a stunning backdrop, sometimes capped with snow. The area was colonized for the first time many centuries ago; Stone Age people settled here, followed in the fourth century BC by the Greeks from Rhodes who gave their settlement the name it – in slightly modified form – bears today. The town coat of arms includes three roses. After the Greeks came the Romans, then the Visigoths. In the Middle Ages, Roses was a base for the Catalan fleet.

From here, over 300 war ships set sail in 1354 to put down a rebellion in Catalan-controlled Sardinia. Roses continued to prosper throughout the 15th century, principally through trading in coral.

If we ignore the promenade for a moment, we see that Roses has a number of interesting sights to show for itself: a large fishing harbour, home to the largest fleet on the Costa Brava, and a surprisingly large selection of excellent restaurants, which attract guests from far afield. Furthermore, the old town and the broad beach with its many water-sports facilities are reason enough for a visit.

SIGHTS

Cabo Falco

Two medieval defence towers, Torre Marina and Torre Mosaica. *On the hill to the east of the town*

Castillo de Trinidad

Old castle, also known as the Castell de la Poncella. Her five cannons were intended as a defence against pirate attack. Not far from the ruins is a lighthouse from which there is a fantastic view. *In the hills to the east of the town*

Castre Visigotic

Here, on top of the 228-m-high *Puig Rom*, stand the ruins of an old Visigoth fortress. The site is easily accessible by car.

Ciutadella

The construction of this huge pentagonal citadel was begun in 1543, at the behest of Charles V. At certain times, more than 2,000 soldiers were stationed here. The fortress was constructed on top of Greek and

Michelin stars

Alongside the Basque region, the Costa Brava and its hinterland is Spain's gourmet paradise. In recent years, more Michelin stars have been awarded in this region than in any other. The "Michelin 2000" commends more than two dozen restaurants, seven of which are in Barcelona. One received two stars, the Sant Pau in Sant Pol near Calella. The El Bulli in Cala Montjoi near Roses and El Racó de Can Fabes in Sant Celoni can even lay claim to three! Certainly two of the best restaurants in Spain.

Roman foundations. During the Napoleonic Wars, the site was plundered and partly demolished by the French. *Monumento Nacional, behind the old town*

Creu d'en Corbatella and Cau de les Guilles

Prehistoric excavation site and dolmen (tomb). Close by are several Visigoth graves and the remains of a church. *On the Puig Rom, to the north of the town (signposted)*

Plaça Catalunya

The main square in Roses deserves mention, though not because of its unspoilt character. This is sadly no longer the case. Nevertheless, it is worth taking a look on a Saturday evening, when people, including complete strangers and passers-by, get together to dance the Sardana. Folklore close up.

Santa Maria de Roses

The original Romanesque church was part of the Benedictine monastery, Montestir dels Benedictins. It was first mentioned in the year 1022, and belonged to an early Christian burial site. The present-day structure dates from 1543. *Situated within the Ciutadella*

RESTAURANTS

Can Ramon

Pretty little restaurant serving only the finest quality fish. Highly recommended. *Carrer Sant Elm, 18; Tel. 972 25 69 18; category 2*

Flor de Lis

French cuisine in the fishing port of Roses! The quality of the fish and other seafood is excellent, for example the sea perch suprême, served with mushroom salad. The restaurant has been awarded a Michelin star and is worth making a detour for – provided you remember to book a table! *Cosconilles, 47; Tel. 972 25 43 16; category 1*

Hacienda El Bulli

★ The best restaurant in Spain, some say in the world! Situated outside the town in the Cala Montjoi. Unique Catalan specialities, such as mushroom carpaccio with potato salad, scorpion fish with pepper, and loin of rabbit with snails. Booking a table is a must! *Daily, except Mon and Tues; Cala Montjoi; Tel. 972 15 04 57; category 1*

El Jabalí

Country-style restaurant in the holiday village of Santa Margarita. *Daily, April–Oct; Platja Salatón; Tel. 972 25 65 25; category 2–3*

La Llar

Situated outside of town in the direction of Figueres, this restaurant has a good selection of fish dishes. Our tip: *Panaché de pescados de mercado* – a selection of fish from the market, prepared in traditional Catalan fashion, with an elegant touch (1 Michelin star). *Closed Wed evenings; Carretera Figueres; Tel. 972 25 53 68; category 1*

Mar y Sol

Cosy little restaurant with small terrace. Great fish and good wine. *Av. de Rhode, s/n; Tel. 972 25 21 15; category 2*

SHOPPING

In addition to the usual selection of tourist shops, there are a number of good suppliers of equipment for diving, fishing and other water sports. On no account should we miss the ★ *fish market (Mon–Fri 5 pm–7 pm)* at the fishing port. Self-caterers can stock up on fish – like the locals – at the excellent fish shops around the harbour. By the way, the bar at the entrance to the harbour serves great fish dishes and is reasonably priced, too.

HOTELS

Almadraba Park

Most attractive hotel with its own pool, tennis courts and a beautiful garden. *60 rooms; closed mid-Oct–mid-April; Platja Almadraba, s/n; Tel. 972 25 65 50; Fax 972 25 67 50; category 1*

Mediterráneo

Highly recommended hotel set directly on the promenade. *48 rooms; Carrer Quevedo, s/n; Tel. 972 25 63 00; Fax 972 25 49 10; category 2*

Novel Risech

Modest, well-run hotel with terrace and fine view. *78 rooms; closed mid-Nov–mid-Dec; Av. de Rhode, 183; Tel. 972 25 62 84; Fax 972 25 68 11; category 3*

Terraza

Large hotel, situated alongside the main beach, with its own pool. *112 rooms; closed Nov–beginning of Holy Week; Passeig Marítim, 16; Tel. 972 25 61 54; Fax 972 25 68 66; category 1*

SPORTS & LEISURE

In and around Roses there are many bays and coves with attractive beaches, including Canyelles Grosses, Cala Mosca, Cala Llado, Cala Murtra, Platja de Santa Margarita, to name but a few, not forgetting the long, wide main beach, Badia de Roses.

Water sports

Club de Mar: sailing (also courses), windsurfing, water-skiing, Grup d'Esports Nàutics, *Moll Comercial (Muelle); Tel. 972 25 70 03;* Poseidon Centro de Buceo: diving (equipment can be rented), *Urb. Santa Margarita, s/n; Tel. 972 25 57 72;* Roses-Sub diving centre: courses in accordance with international guidelines, *Eugeni d'Ors, 15; Tel. 972 25 52 69*

INFORMATION

Oficina Municipal de Turisme

Av. de Rhode, 101; Tel. 972 25 73 31; Fax 972 15 11 50

SURROUNDING AREA

Walking in the mountains

In the vicinity of Roses there are many footpaths through the neighbouring hills; in general they are not too steep and the views afforded are – weather permitting – breathtaking. To the east of Roses is the 228-m-high *Puig Rom*. From the top you have a splendid panorama across the bay and the ruins of a Visigoth fortress and the Castillo de la Trinidad. The climb up ✿ *El Pení* is best tackled as part of a longer hike $(2-2^1/_2$ hrs). Set off from Roses in a north-easterly direction, via Mas Rahola, Puig de l'Aliga and Puig Alt. Your destination, El Pení, is 605 m high. From the summit the view across to Cap de Creus is fantastic. You can continue your walk down to Cadaqués – total walking time from Roses is almost three hours – and return with the bus or by boat.

Castelló d'Empúries   (100/C5)
This very pretty medieval town (pop. 2,500) lies to the west of Empúriabrava, and provides a welcome contrast to the resorts on the coast. It was at one time the seat of the Count of Empúries and was also a bishopric as far back as the eighth century. The 13th-century cathedral of Santa Maria is of particular interest, having a splendid marble portal depicting the 12 apostles and a Romanesque bell tower. Inside, the high altar is Gothic. The Museo Parroquial contains the elaborate 15th-century retable carved by Vicente Borras. *Information: Oficina de Turisme, Plaça dels Homes, 1; Tel. 972 15 62 33*

Empúriabrava   (101/D5)
A modern holiday village to the south of Roses, which has somewhat broken the mould of the run-of-the-mill developments

so typical of the Costa Brava. It lies between an extensive, well-tended sandy beach and the rivers Salines and Muga, and is criss-crossed by numerous small canals. The planner's concept envisaged almost every holiday apartment having its own landing stage. There is also a marina and you can take boat trips along the 30-km-long network of canals. Empúriabrava also offers many discotheques, excellent water-skiing facilities and the opportunity to sail, surf and dive. There is an airfield, a firing range and the largest parachutist's club in Europe. Admittedly, this is not the place to come if you're looking just to get away from it all. *Information: Urb. Empúriabrava; Tel. 972 45 08 02*

Palau Saverdera   (101/D4)
The ruins of an old castle, which was first mentioned in AD 822, are to be found to the north of Rodes. Remains of an old 12th-century monastery, annexed to nearby Sant Pere de Rodes. The vaults today house a restaurant, *Rhodas Palau (Tel. 972 55 20 62; category 2)*.

Parc Natural dels Aiguamolls de l'Empordà   (100–101/C–D5–6)
★ Catalonia's largest expanse of marshland is one of the most fascinating wetland habitats in the Mediterranean region and a breeding ground for thousands of waterfowl. Don't forget to bring your binoculars with you, so that you can observe the birds without disturbing them. *Visitor's centre El Cortalet on the road from Castelló d'Empúries to Sant Pere Pescador; Tel. 972 45 42 22*

The heart of the Costa Brava

*Medieval towns, cork oak groves
and first-rate fish cuisine*

This central section of the Costa Brava, between L'Estartit and Palamós, is its heartland – and a little on the fat side at that. The unspoilt appearance of this breathtaking landscape is interrupted here and there by multi-storeyed monuments to the gods of commerce. As if to give you a taste of what awaits you further south. Don't be put off straight away – reality will hit you in the face soon enough. Instead, open your eyes to the fascinating old towns, the wild coves cutting deep into the coastline, the traces of Spain's earliest inhabitants. Will people marvel at today's concrete structures in 2,500 years? By the time you've savoured the second bottle of Vina Sol at the most beautiful hotel on the coast, you'll have forgotten all about this question. Next morning, you'll be sad to leave and look forward eagerly to the rest of your journey, through

dark forests of cork oak, the clear blue sky above you. And you'll be grateful for a glimpse now and then of the miracle that is the Costa Brava – the wild coast.

L'ESTARTIT

(105/E-F3) L'Estartit has two faces, or rather three, in fact. Firstly, there's the wonderful 3-km-long beach and behind it the small harbour. Then there are a few apartment blocks at the southern end of the Platja. Finally, there is the romantic old town, a few kilometres away from the holiday hustle and bustle. Why? Local government administration divides L'Estartit (pop. 700) into two separate villages: the old royal seat of Torroella de Montgrí (pop. 4,500) and the smartened-up former fishing village by the sea. Opposites that complement each other. L'Estartit is not one of those typically dreadful tourist traps, and although hordes of multi-national visitors are seen to march up and down the promenade and pedestrian precinct in summer, they seldom get as far as the streets of

*All's right with the world
in idyllic Calella de Palafrugell:
clear water, pretty bays and
a captivating view*

Torroella. And so this two-in-one town offers the best of both worlds: excitement and a peaceful idyll.

SIGHTS

Casa de Villa
Old Town Hall on the *Plaça de la Vila* in the centre of Torroella. Built in the 14th century. Includes the ancient Capella de Sant Antoni del Porquet.

Castillo de Montgrí
⬥ Between Torroella and L'Estartit stands the 300-m-high mountain Montgrí. At the end of the 13th century, King Jaime II of Aragón and Catalonia, who had chosen Torroella as one of his official residences, built a castle here to guard against the predatory Counts of Empúries. After a roughly one-hour climb, you come across an impressive complex of walls and round towers. Admittedly, only the outer walls can be seen, since the rest was never completed. Splendid view of the coast and hinterland.

Ermita de Santa Catalina
Fourteenth-century pilgrimage chapel adjacent to the King's castle. Every November, thousands of the faithful make their way here from L'Estartit and Torroella.

Iglesia Parroquial
Beautiful Gothic parish church, also on the *Plaça de la Vila* in Tor-

MARCO POLO SELECTION:
CENTRAL COSTA BRAVA

1 Amateur rock in Begur
A courtyard, a warm evening, rock music blasting from the loudspeakers till the walls vibrate (page 66)

2 Fish at Sa Punta in Platja de Pals
You must try the monk fish and potato stew. Book a table! (page 67)

3 Sacred Girona
Mount the steps up to the cathedral: an awe-inspiring sight. Gaze down on the old town and the river (page 69)

4 The ancient Iberians in Ullastret
Old friends from the Asterix comics, but how did they really live? Pay them a visit in 2,500-year-old Ullastret (page 67)

5 Sunday is Market Day
It's Sunday in Palafrugell. Women man the stalls and the men drink *vi negre* (page 73)

6 The Russian Park
About 80 years ago, a Russian came to Calella de Palafrugell, bringing a few plants with him ... (page 73)

roella. The façade dates from the 16th century. In front of the church is a garden containing remnants of the old city wall.

Iglesia Santa Ana
Parish church of L'Estartit, containing a statue of St Anne in a side chapel. She is represented holding her hand over the head of the young Jesus. *Centre of L'Estartit*

Palacio Marqués de Robert
Palatial town house from the Renaissance period, with an impressive façade and a very beautiful inner courtyard, incorporating a well and a fine flight of steps. Built for one of the noble families of Torroella. *Town centre (signposted)*

Portal de Santa Caterina
One of Torroella's four old city gates, a square tower with battlements. Of the four defensive towers, only the round Torre de les Bruixes (the witches' tower) still stands. A diagram shows the extent of the original fortifications. *On the road towards Verges*

MUSEUMS

Museu del Montgrí i del Baix Ter – Casa Pastors
Exhibition of regional culture, housed in a medieval town house in Torroella. *Carrer Major, 31; daily, except Sun, 10 am–2 pm and 6 pm–9 pm, closed Oct–April; admission: 250 ptas*

Sala d'Exposiciones Capella de Sant Antoni
Thirteenth-century Gothic chapel with façade added in the 18th century. Probably the first church to be built in Torroella. It has also been used to stage temporary exhibitions. *Plaça de la Vila*

RESTAURANTS

Can Cervera
Pleasant *tapas* bar in the pedestrian precinct in L'Estartit. A range of over 20 different appetizers is always on the menu. *Carrer Santa Ana, 25; category 2*

Castillo del Misterio
Castle in Torroella with haunted restaurant and a magician to bewitch you during your meal. *Carrer de l'Església, 10; Tel. 972 75 08 15; category 2*

Eden
Gourmet restaurant, but don't be put off by the setting – in a tourist high-rise block – because the traditional Catalan specialities, such as *pollastre amb musclos* (chicken with mussels), are excellent. *Victor Concas, 2; Tel. 972 75 21 34; category 1*

Elias
Restaurant with a good menu and 15 guest rooms. *Carrer Major, 24; Tel. 972 75 80 09; category 3*

La Gaviota
The view of the beach is included in the price at "The Seagull" fish restaurant. *Closed Mon evenings and Nov; Passeig Marítim, 92; Tel. 972 75 20 19; category 2*

Rosamar
Recommended restaurant on the promenade at L'Estartit, serving both fish and meat dishes. *Passeig Marítim, 45; Tel. 972 75 14 43; category 2*

Las Salinas
The best fish restaurant in L'Estartit. *Passeig Molinet, 5; Tel. 972 75 16 11; category 1*

Santa Ana

Standard restaurant with a special extra, namely the daily vegetarian menu. *Santa Ana, 55; no Tel.; category 3*

Els Tascon

Pleasant restaurant offering regional specialities, also on the terrace. *Open May–Sept only; Roca-Maura-Edificio Medas Park II; Tel. 972 75 12 87; category 2*

SHOPPING

El Bronce

Here you get hand-made jewellery with South American inspired designs. *Torroella, Carrer Major, 51*

Dulcería Batlle

This cake shop, established in 1880, is a paradise for visitors with a sweet tooth. *Torroella, Carrer de Ulla, 6*

Mar del Coral

How about this unusual idea for a souvenir: preserved sea creatures, such as fish, starfish, and corals, are sold here. *Carrer Santa Ana, 68*

Weekly markets

Torroella: Monday, succulent fruit and fresh vegetables. L'Estartit *(Carrer de Eivissa)*: Thursdays, fish!

HOTELS

Bell Aire

The best hotel in town. *76 rooms; closed Oct–March; Carrer de L'Església, 39; Tel. 972 75 13 02; Fax 972 75 19 58; category 2*

Hotel Les Illes

This hotel is ideal for divers; diving centre. *18 rooms; March–Oct; Carrer Illes, 55 (to the rear of the harbour); Tel. 972 75 12 39; category 3*

The small harbour reflects the prettier side of L'Estartit

Miramar

This hotel certainly has character – plus a swimming pool, a slightly overgrown garden and tennis courts! *64 rooms; closed Oct–April; Av. de Roma, 13–21; Tel. 972 75 06 28; Fax 972 75 05 00; category 1*

SPORTS & LEISURE

L'Estartit's beautiful beach offers countless opportunities for water-sports fans. It is also ideal for families with children, since it slopes gently down into the water.

Water sports

Club Náutico Estartit, *Passeig Marítim; Tel. 972 75 14 02,* and La Sirena Diving Club, *Passeig Marítim; Tel. 972 75 09 54*

Golf

Club de Golf de Pals, 18 km from Torroella, 18 holes. *Tel. 972 63 60 06.* Golfing equipment can be rented at the course.

Horse riding

Equitación mas Paguina, Carretera de la Gola, no Tel.

Tennis

Urb. Torre Gran; Tel. 972 75 84 54

Walking

There are many well-marked paths and trails in the area. Look out for the coloured arrows. *For more information, ask at the Oficina de Turisme*

ENTERTAINMENT

There is a good choice of ✭ discotheques in L'Estartit, which are open till dawn in the summer months (*Genesis, Carrer de Illes, 27,* and *Ola Ola, Carrer de l'incora, s/n*). Almost next door, on the *Carrer d'Eivissa (No. 40 onwards),* is a huge amusement centre packed with bars and pubs, plus a café aimed mainly at young people and fans of extremely loud music! For the more sensitive guest, there are other alternatives, such as:

Can Fonsu

❖ Bar, close to the Torroella tourist information centre. Also a good place to rub shoulders with the locals. *Av. Lluís Companys, 56*

Fancy-Bar

Small bar attached to a garden restaurant. *L'Estartit, Carrer d'Eivissa, 3*

Look

Billiard bar in Torroella. *Passeig de Catalunya*

Montserrat

✭ Café with a good selection of long drinks. Ideal for those long summer evenings in L'Estartit. *Passeig Marítim, 36*

INFORMATION

L'Estartit:
Oficina Municipal de Turisme
Passeig Marítim, 33; Tel. 972 75 19 10; Fax 972 75 17 49

Torroella de Montgrí:
Oficina Municipal de Turisme
Av. Lluís Companys, 51; Tel. 972 75 83 00; Fax 972 76 02 36

SURROUNDING AREA

Begur   (105/F5)

One of the prettiest towns on the Costa Brava (pop. 3,000), Begur's medieval houses and streets cluster

Aiguablava Bay, probably the most beautiful on the Costa Brava

round the foot of a hill on top of which stand the ruins of a fortress. Built to ward off pirate raids, destroyed in 1456 and subsequently rebuilt, the castle, in its elevated position high over the coast, affords a magnificent view of the surrounding countryside. In the town itself is the *Galeria d'Art Can Marc*, showing contemporary Catalan art in the *Carrer Creu*. Begur is an ideal spot for an evening stroll. Weekend tip: ★ ❂ ⚡ amateur rock bands play live in the pretty inner courtyard of the *Bar C. Roack, Musical*, just 30 m from the main car park.

Bellcaire d'Empordà (105/D3)
This very old village of just 500 souls lies to the west of L'Estartit and was first mentioned in AD 881. The Romanesque parish church was even named in the Papal Bull issued by Sylvester II in 1002. Take a closer look at the Castell-Palau de Bellcaire, a mighty fortress with four towers.

Aiguablava Bay (105/F5)
〰 Probably the most beautiful bay along the Costa Brava, lying south of Begur. No picture post-

card can really do justice to the turquoise of the sea and the rich green of the pine trees. The residential areas around the bay, with their noble villas, have a certain flair, similar to that on the Côte d'Azur. Add to this the best hotel in the region: the *Aigua Blava (90 rooms; closed Nov–Feb; Playa de Fornells; Tel. 972 62 20 58; Fax 972 62 21 12)*, a luxury establishment in park-like grounds with a swimming pool, tennis courts, a miniature golf course and a landing stage. The accommodation is outstanding, the restaurant first-class – hardly surprising that the Rothschilds and the Aga Khan have been known to stay here. This hotel certainly deserves the classification "Luxury", so early booking is essential. If you don't manage to get a room here, try the 〰 *Parador Costa Brava (83 rooms; Tel. 972 62 21 62; Fax 972 62 21 66; category 1)*, situated on the other side of the bay – where the view is even better.

Illes Medes (105/F3)
Totally unspoilt, this group of islands lies directly opposite the beach at L'Estartit. Meda Gran, the largest island, was often used as a

hiding place by Norman, Algerian and Turkish pirates. Later, in the 15th century, monks built a fortified monastery here. During the Napoleonic Wars, the British seized the islands, only to be driven out by the French. The Illes Medes have been uninhabited since 1890 (except for the lighthouse), hence an unusually rich flora and fauna has managed to establish itself. So-called "aquarium boats", with glass panels in the hull, bring visitors in just a few minutes from L'Estartit to marvel at the underwater world.

Pals (105/E4)
↘↗ Small village (pop. 1,700) to the south of Torroella and once more you're transported back to the Middle Ages. Much of the original tenth-century settlement (on the hill above the newer part of the village) has been lovingly and painstakingly restored: fortifications, houses, winding streets, towers and the Town Hall. From up here, you have a fine view over the plain with its rice plantations. We recommend a visit in the evening, when the street lights cast a characteristic glow and a few restaurants entice you to dine.

Platja de Pals (105/F4)
Five kilometres from Pals is the beach Platja de Pals, in a fine, sandy bay. A new holiday village has been built, mainly consisting of villas and luxury apartments. ★ Restaurant: Sa Punta (Urb. Sa Punta, Platja de Pals; daily, except Mon, closed mid-Jan–mid-Feb; Tel. 972 66 73 76; Fax 972 66 73 15; category 1), one of the finest fish restaurants on the coast. Speciality of the house: Suquet marinero de rape con patatas tiernas (monkfish and potato stew). Don't

forget to book a table! Twenty-two luxurious hotel rooms.

Peratallada (105/D4)
Another small, medieval town a few kilometres inland, southwest of Torroella. There's lots to see – the ruined city wall, the town houses of patricians and other wealthy citizens, cobbled streets bursting with life. No stuffy museum atmosphere here, but a genuine, lived-in one. Well worth a visit.

Ullastret (105/D4)
★ One of the highlights of any trip to the Costa Brava is a visit to Ullastret (pop. 500). Here is the site of the ancient Iberian settlement, the *Poblat Ibèric*, so to speak the home of the original inhabitants of Spain. The Celtiberians arrived on the Iberian peninsula around the turn of the seventh century BC. In about 600 BC they began to build a settlement on a hill in the middle of what was a lake (now dried up), the water affording them some protection from attack. To the east, the weak point in this defence, they constructed mighty ramparts with watchtowers, but also incorporating facilities for water and grain storage. The Iberians probably copied many of the technical innovations brought in to the country by the Greeks, who had meanwhile established a port at Emporion (20 km away). The two communities traded with each other on a large scale, proof being the many Greek coins and items of pottery found here in Ullastret. About 200 BC the Iberians joined forces with Rome's arch enemy Carthage to attack Roman forces on the peninsula. Unfortunately, the all-powerful Roman war ma-

The archaeological museum in Ullastret

chine was too much for the Iberians and their settlement at Ullastret was literally overrun and subsequently abandoned. The Iberians probably threw in their lot with the Greeks and lived happily ever after. A museum, erected on the site of the old acropolis documents the unique history of Ullastret. Its exhibits, alongside coins, ceramics, weapons and other artefacts, include a piece of written evidence of the time, inscribed with Iberian characters. The contents of this document remain a mystery, since the 28 characters of the Iberian language have yet to be deciphered. *Tues–Sun 10.30 am–1 pm and 4 pm–8 pm; in winter, Tues–Sun 10 am–12 am and 4 pm–6 pm*

GIRONA

(104/A4–5) The outskirts of the capital of the province of Girona are just as awful as those of any other southern town. Too much traffic, industry, run-down shopping centres. It makes you want to turn back, but don't, otherwise you'll miss one of the most intact old town centres in Spain. Girona, with its 87,000 inhabitants, is pure Middle Ages. If you're tired of the milling masses and the smell of sun-tan lotion at the coast, then travel the 35 km to Girona for a few hours or an evening away from it all. A typical southern European city at last, with 2,500 years of colourful history, strategically located at the confluence of the rivers Ter and Onyar and on the major north-south route across the Pyrenees. The Iberians, Romans, Visigoths, Arabs and Charlemagne and his Franks have all left their mark on this metropolis. Even Napoleon, who besieged the city for seven months in 1809, pronounced it "immortal".

Old University

The university of Girona was founded in 1443. In the courtyard, remains of the old Roman city wall can be seen. *Plaça de Sant Domènec, s/n*

Old town

Lies to the east of the Riu Onyar: cobbled streets, well-trodden steps, houses huddled together – a fascinating backdrop for a walk.

Banys Arabs – the Arabian baths

Public baths, built by Christians in the North African style as late as the 13th century, 400 years after the Moors had been driven out of Girona. *Carrer Rei Ferran el Catòlic; Tues–Sat 10 am–1 pm and 4.30 pm–7 pm, Sun 10.30 am–1 pm*

Carrer dels Alemanys

Street of the Germans, behind the *Plaça de Sant Domènec.* This is where a barracks was built in the 17th

68

century to accommodate German mercenaries, brought in to protect the city against the French.

Casa Agullana
Magnificent 17th-century house, one of the most-photographed buildings in Girona. *To the southwest of the Plaça de Sant Domènec*

Fontana d'Or
Medieval patrician's residence with some late Romanesque elements. *Carrer Ciutadans*

Call Jueu – Jewish Quarter
From the 9th to the 15th century, Girona's old Jewish Quarter, "el call", was situated around the *Carrer de la Força.* Here was also the home of the Jewish scholar Isaac el Cec (Isaac the Blind) in the Middle Ages.

Cathedral
★ One of the most beautiful sacred buildings in Spain, originally founded, it is said, by Charlemagne. A Romanesque church was consecrated on this site in 1038, parts of which survive today. Numerous additions have been made to the cathedral over the centuries, in a variety of architectural styles. An endless flight of steps (17th century) leads up to the portal. The huge, present-day nave was completed in 1604, the tower, crowned by the figure of an angel, in 1580. The Baroque façade was added in 1733. The trapezoidal cloisters with their richly decorated capitals and friezes date from the 12th century. In the Romanesque chancel is a marble altar from 1038 and a bishop's throne from the same period. The cathedral museum, the *Tresoro*, is situated in

three of the five chapter houses off the left-hand aisle. Alongside priceless examples of the goldsmith's art and numerous Romanesque and Gothic sculptures, is probably the most valuable sacred treasure in Spain, the *Tapiz de la Creación*, a huge, roughly 900-year-old wall hanging, depicting the creation story. *Plaça de la Catedral; Tues–Sat 10 am–1 pm and 4.30 pm–7 pm, Sun 10 am–1 pm*

Passeig Reina Joana
Splendid walkway along the old city walls.

Sant Feliu
Three-nave church in Gothic style, below the cathedral. It is said that the oldest parts stand on the catacombs where Sant Narcís was murdered in the fourth century. The church is dedicated to Sant Feliu, who was Bishop of Girona in the fourth century. He, too, died a martyr's death. The grave of Sant Narcís and other early Christian sarcophagi can be seen in the interior.

Sant Mari
Tenth-century monastery, which was completely rebuilt in the 17th century as a Jesuit abbey. *Plaça de Sant Domènec*

Torre Gironella
⚐ Mighty fortified tower, part of the Roman/medieval fortifications of Girona. From the top of the tower, you have a panoramic view across part of the old town. *East of the cathedral*

Episcopal Palace – Museu d'Art
Linked to the cathedral by an archway, this 12th-century ecclesiasti-

Flight of steps next to the Casa Agullana in Girona

cal court now houses the diocesan museum with exhibits from early Christian times to the present day, for example, the St Michael altarpiece and documents belonging to the painter Goya. *Pujada de la Catedral 14; Tues–Sat 10 am–1 pm and 4.30 pm–7 pm, Sun 10 am–1 pm; admission: 250 ptas*

Sant Pere de Galligants

Romanesque church that houses the Museu d'Arqueologia. Here, you can see prehistoric, Greek, Carthaginian and Roman finds from the region. *Carrer Santa Lúcia, 1; Tues–Sat 10 am–1 pm and 4.30 pm–7 pm; admission: 200 ptas*

RESTAURANTS

Albereda

The best restaurant in town, offering superb Catalan specialities.*Closed Mon evenings; Albereda, 7; Tel. 972 22 60 02; category 2*

El Celler de Can Roca

The previous restaurant, "Pepita", run by the Roca family, was very popular and the same is true of this one, with its wide-ranging menu, which was awarded one Michelin star. Outside town, towards Olot. *Closed Sun and Mon; Carretera Taial, 40; Tel. 972 22 21 57; category 1*

Selva Mar

This restaurant specializes in fish and mussel dishes. *Santa Eugnia, 81; Tel. 972 23 63 29; category 2*

SHOPPING

Take the time to wander around the shops – some of them centuries' old – especially if you're a collector of antiques and old books.

HOTELS

Bellmirall

Elegant B&B with seven highly original bedrooms. *Bellmirall 3; Tel. 972 20 40 09; category 2*

Meliá Confort Girona

The largest hotel in Girona. *114 rooms; Carretera Barcelona, 112; Tel. 972 40 05 00; Fax 972 24 32 33; category 1*

ENTERTAINMENT

Why not take an evening stroll through the old town or along the *Rambla de la Llibertat* with its

70

cafés and elegant shops – you may even come across a group dancing the Sardana.

Oficina Municipal de Turisme
Rambla de la Llibertat, 1; Tel. 972 22 65 75; Fax 972 22 66 12; www.ddgi.es

PALAMÓS

(**109/F2**) It would be wrong to describe Palamós (pop. 13,000) as merely a tourist destination. Firstly, owing to the discreet development of the tourist infrastructure around an intact old town (although the skyline along the beautiful beach is dominated by high-rise hotel blocks), and secondly, to the economic activities of the town. Palamós boasts an important fishing harbour and marina with boatbuilders' workshops. The commercial harbour is also devoted to the once-flourishing cork industry (there are numerous cork oak plantations in this part of the Costa Brava).

Admittedly, the harbour at Palamós enjoyed its "golden age" several centuries ago. It was extended in 1277 to faciliate the export of cork, and it was from here that the Catalan fleet put out to conquer Sicily in 1299. In 1526 the pirate Barbarossa – who was later to sack Cadaqués – landed here and left his bloody mark on the town. The second fleet to set sail from Palamós was the Armada of the Catholic king of Spain in 1571. In an encounter off Lepanto she shot to pieces the allegedly invincible Turkish fleet. Cervantes, the author of *Don Quixote*, lost a hand in the battle. He was taken prisoner and is said to have spent five years in slavery in Algeria. The harbour was destroyed during the Spanish Civil War; the town, too, suffered some damage. The old town remained intact and is so today – despite the growing tourist industry.

Monument "A la gent del Mar"
The sculpture by Joan Abres (1990) on the *Passeig del Mar* represents fishermen and their wives carrying home their catch in baskets on their heads.

Iglesia Santa Maria
Gothic parish church of Palamós, consecrated in 1371. It was destroyed by Turkish pirates but later rebuilt in the 16th century. Inside, reredos in the style of the Flemish School. The Museu Parroquial Mossén Pau is also housed here. *Plaça Santa Maria*

Punta del Castell
Remains of an Iberian settlement to the north of *Platja de La Fosca.*

Punta del Moli
✲ Promontory with lighthouse *in the south of Palamós.* Magnificent view.

Museu Cau de la Costa Brava
Archaeological and folkloristic collection, including Palamós's coins from the 15th century. *Carrer Enric Vincke, s/n; daily, 10 am– 1 pm and 4 pm–6.30 pm; admission: 250 ptas*

RESTAURANTS

L'Art
High-quality, creative fish cuisine. *Closed Thurs evenings, Sun evenings and Jan; Passeig del Mar, 7; Tel. 972 31 55 32; category 2*

El Campanar
❖ Bar in the vaults next to the parish church. *Carrer de les Notaries, 20; category 3*

La Cuineta
Good range of fish dishes. *Open 15 June–15 Sept only; Adri n Alvarez, 111; Tel. 972 31 40 01; category 2*

La Gamba
One of the finest and most traditional fish restaurants, though a bit on the touristy side, perhaps. *Closed Wed; Plaça Sant Pere; Tel. 972 31 46 33; category 2*

Maria de Cadaqués
❖ First-class fish restaurant. *Daily, except Mon, closed 15 Dec– 15 Jan; Notaries, 39; Tel. 972 31 40 09; category 2*

SHOPPING

The old town is brimming with shops selling cork products. Visit the weekday market at 5 pm in *La Llotja*, the auction hall at the fishing harbour.

HOTELS

Marina
Medium-standard accommodation. *62 rooms; closed 24–31 Dec; Av. 11 de Setembre, 48; Tel. 972 31 42 50; Fax 972 60 00 24; category 2*

Trias
Luxury hotel with swimming pool, at the beach. *70 rooms; closed 6 Oct–25 March; Passeig del Mar; Tel. 972 60 18 00; Fax 972 60 18 19; category 1*

Vostra Llar
Well-appointed hotel. *45 rooms; closed Nov–March; Av. President Maci, 12; Tel. 972 31 42 62; Fax 972 31 43 07; category 2*

SPORTS & LEISURE

Sailing
In 1992, the Olympic sailing competitions took place off Palamós. Club de Vela Palamós; *Puerto Zona Deportiva; Tel. 972 31 58 71*

Tennis
Club Tenis Llafranc, with large sports complex including 19 courts, a swimming pool, a restaurant and a football pitch. Guests welcome. *Tel. 972 30 23 08*

Water sports
Tramontana Surf, where surfing and sailing equipment can be rented. Courses available. *Carrer Aubi, 22; Tel. 972 30 10 74*

ENTERTAINMENT

Palamós has several beach discotheques, and in July stages the Festival Internacional de Música. The *Xivarri* is more than just a restaurant – dine to the strains of "habaneras".

INFORMATION

Oficina Municipal d'Informació Turística
Passeig del Mar; Tel. 972 60 05 00; Fax 972 60 01 37

La Bisbal   (104/C4)

Old diocesan town of 7,500 inhabitants, to the north of Palamós, and the centre of the Catalan ceramics industry. Countless workshops, small factories and shops supplying anything from kitsch to fine art. Bisbal is also the site of Spain's leading art college specializing in ceramics. The name of the town comes from the Catalan word for bishop; Emperor Charles the Bald is said to have presented Bisbal to the Bishopric of Girona as a gift. In the Middle Ages, the church dignitaries resided in the Castillo-Palacio Episcopal, an old castle. The Torre de Homenaje (Tower of Homage) dates from the 13th century.

Calella de Palafrugell   (105/F6)

Idyllic fishing village, to the north of Palamós, where all is more or less right with the world: clean water, pretty bays and a fabulous botanical garden, the ★ *Jardín de los Rusos*. It was created in 1923 by an exiled Russian officer on Cap Roig, 4 km outside the town, and is a treasure-trove of over 100 species of fragrant Mediterranean plants and flowers. In summer, the town comes alive to the sound of the Cantadas de Habaneras – a competition between singers of the traditional Cuban-influenced blues. Fuelled by a good dose of Cremat (a mixture of coffee, rum and herbs), the competitors intone melancholy songs of their faraway homeland and the big, wide world. *Recommended hotel: Sant Roc (42 rooms; Pl. Atlántic, 2; Tel. 972 61 42 50; Fax 972 61 40 68; category 2)*, a most attractive, traditional hotel with sea view.

Calonge   (109/E2)

Medieval village to the west of Palamós (pop. 5,000, including surrounding hamlets). A massive, 12th-century fortress, Castillo de Sessa, dominates the village.

Dolmen de la
Cova d'en Daina   (109/D2)

Impressive Stone Age burial site, west of Palamós, including several megalithic graves thought to be about 4,000 years old. Close to the mountain village of Romanya de la Selva.

Llafranc   (105/F6)

Four kilometres down the coast from Calella is Llafranc, set in a delightful bay. There are no high-rise hotels here, just a few magnificent villas. Unfortunately the main road runs directly alongside the beach.

Palafrugell   (105/E5)

This small, industrial town (pop. 14,000) would not normally warrant a mention, were it not for the old Moorish city wall that encloses the historical town centre. Be sure to visit the bacchanalian ★ Sunday market, where you can sample a few glasses of *vi negre*. Don't overdo it though, it's fairly strong stuff – 17 per cent proof! Follow it up with some lamb at *Mas Oliver (Creu Roqui Òola; Tel. 972 30 10 41; category 2)* – a must for all fans of Catalan cuisine.

Tamariu   (105/F5)

Fabulous beach to the north of Calella and Llafranc – maybe a glimpse of paradise. Just an unspoilt fishing village with charming restaurants. That's why most people don't bother to hang around for very long.

Tourism for the masses on the wild coast

Water sports and endless nights for international guests – young people drawn to the discos and the beach

Positively speaking, this is where the dazzling part of the Costa Brava begins: endless nights, a fast and furious lifestyle – at least for as long as the holiday lasts. Here are the high-rise blocks and tourist bunkers of Manhattan on the Med. The beach is just one endless party – well, almost. *Viva la Ilusión!*

In actual fact the true Costa Brava lies here in front of you – the wild coast, in the truest sense of the word – from Platja d'Aro to Lloret. You can't miss it. The signs are unmistakable. Behind almost every fabulous bay, an enormous, concrete monument to mass tourism towers into the sky. But then, the next idyllic cove is just around the corner and you are granted a moment's respite.

The Costa Brava, the most-visited stretch of coastline along the Mediterranean. This means, of course, precisely this southern section. Forty years of unrestrain-

The tourist centre Blanes has managed to retain its old fishing harbour and daily fish auction

ed expansion in the tourist industry have given rise to a situation that is deplored by many guests and quite a number of their hosts, too. In recent years, opinions have been changing on this stretch of the Costa Brava. Towns such as Sant Feliu de Guíxols or Tossa de Mar, with their old town centres and (almost) high-rise-free promenades, are refreshing, if rare, exceptions to the rule.

Who cares? It is precisely the younger guests who seem to feel at home on the beaches, walled in by giant concrete hives, buzzing with thousands of tourists. As long as there's a disco, chips and a hamburger to be had, that's fine by them. In amongst all this, you will still find some things that compensate for the hurly-burly: here and there, a tiny, unspoilt cove, an isolated abbey, a peaceful, starlit evening on the beach. A small fish restaurant, perhaps, where the menu is still written in Spanish and you can enjoy a chilled glass of white wine from Perelada. In short, a few of those small blessings the south can reward us with. You'll find them. Even here.

LLORET DE MAR

(108/B–C5) After the idyll of Tossa, Lloret comes as something of a shock. The population jumps to 120,000 in summer, and the town boasts the highest proportion of discotheques in Europe and the second-highest proportion of hotels in Spain (after Madrid). Lloret also looks back on over 2,000 years of history, but you wouldn't think so to look at it. The Iberians settled here, so too the Romans. In the Middle Ages, Italian seafarers set up a colony here. In more recent times, bulldozers moved in, in the name of tourism: "higher" and "louder" are the keys to success here. The former Spanish old town reverberates to the sound of English, German, Dutch and Scandinavian voices. Fishermen have turned to bar- and hotel-keeping. To quote the popular Lloret postcards: "Spain is a madhouse and Lloret is its headquarters!" But times are changing, it seems. The town council has built a sewage plant, and planning permission for further holiday villages is no longer being granted. A change of heart at last?

SIGHTS

Cementiri (Lloret cemetery)
Situated on the road leading to the motorway, it features many monuments in the Catalan Art Nouveau style. *Av. de les Ale-gries/Camí del Repos*

Font de Canaletes
Reproduction of the famous Rambla fountain in Barcelona. *On the promenade*

Sant Roman
Gothic parish church dating from the 15th century. Note the coloured roof tiles. *Plaça de la Església*

Sardana Monument
Sculpture of a dancing couple, on the promenade. *Passeig de la Caleta*

Lloret Castle
Mighty fort with walls and towers, at the northern end of the beach. A well-preserved specimen? Don't be fooled too easily: a rich businessman had it built in 1929 to fulfil a childhood dream. *Sa Caleta*

Sepulcro Romà
Remains of a Roman burial site. *Carretera Urb. Roca Grossa*

MUSEUMS

Believe it or not, there are some!

Centro Cultural Badaguer
Alternating art history exhibitions in a magnificent villa with mosaic floors. Not exactly overrun by visitors. *Passeig Cinto Verdaguer, s/n; Mon–Sat 11 am–1 pm and 5 pm– 10 pm; free admission*

Museu de Lloret de Mar
Municipal museum, documenting the history of Lloret, including archaeological finds. *Carrer de Sant Carles, 16; Mon–Sat 10 am–1 pm and 4 pm–7 pm; admission: 200 ptas*

RESTAURANTS

Lloret is bursting with places to eat out, the choice – for what it's worth – is yours. Here are a few typical Catalan restaurants, of which there are not many:

Ca l'Avi
❧ For generations, the "Grandfather's House" has been a popular destination for the locals. Fresh fish and high-quality meat dishes. *Closed mid-Dec–mid-Jan; Av. de Vidreres, 30; Tel. 97236 53 55; category 2*

Can Bolet
Serves fish and seafood. *Closed Sun evenings and Mon; Sant Mateu, 12; Tel. 972 37 12 37; category 3*

El Celler del Stop
❧ Small pub with reasonably priced menu. Rub shoulders with the locals. *Carrer Puntaires, 17; Tel. 972 36 90 08; category 3*

Les Petxines
This restaurant is living proof that you can dine in style even in a madhouse like Lloret. Excellent fish and one Michelin star to prove it. *Closed Wed; in the Hotel Excelsior, Passeig Mossèn J. Verdaguer, 16; Tel. 972 36 41 37; category 1*

El Rincón de San Cristóbal
❧ Simple fish restaurant in the new district, superb Catalan specialities. No tourists. *Carrer de Tarragona, 24; no Tel.; category 2*

El Trull
For an evening to remember. Enjoy top-quality fish cuisine in stylish surroundings. *3 km outside Lloret, in the Urb. Playa Canyelles; Tel. 972 36 49 28; category 1*

SHOPPING

Art Plaça
Ceramics from the hands of skilled craftsmen, and by Lloret de Mar standards, very tasteful, too. *Plaça de la Església*

Centro Comercial Caravela
Shopping centre at the start of the promenade, with boutiques and shops on several floors. Extravagant swimwear at Tingo Tango on the first floor. *Passeig Agusti Font*

MARCO POLO SELECTION: SOUTH COAST

1 Fish at Hispania
A new star in the restaurant heavens over the Costa Brava. Speciality: crayfish (page 79)

2 The botanical garden at Blanes
A touch of green works wonders after so much concrete. An eldorado for flora fans with its 4,000 or so species of plant (page 79)

3 Pure Costa Brava along the coast road
Car journey from Sant Feliude Guíxols to Tossa de Mar. Fantastic panorama from the winding road (page 85)

4 Tossa de Mar
A walk through the expertly renovated medieval old town to get a stunning view of the town and nearby bays (page 86)

Fabregas
This in an almost 100-year-old shoe shop, which is not exactly inexpensive! Quality does indeed have its price. *Plaça de la Església, s/n*

Weekly market
Worth a visit. Every Tuesday near the casino. You shouldn't miss it! *Daily, until 2 pm; on the Carrer Senia de Rabic*

HOTELS

Lloret has over 200 hotels, which can cater for over 30,000 guests – not including the holiday villages and apartment blocks. Here are just four, not exactly typical, hotels to consider:

Gran Hotel Monterrey
Luxury hotel with a swimming pool, tennis courts and a pleasant park. *228 rooms; closed Dec–March; Carretera de Tossa de Mar, s/n; Tel. 972 36 40 50; Fax 972 36 35 12; category 1*

Neptuno
Ideal if you're just passing through and your finances are limited. *39 rooms; Carrer Josep Lluhi, 11; Tel. 972 36 40 89; category 3*

Roger de Flor
Lloret's "Grand Hotel" with park, swimming pool and tennis courts. *87 rooms; Turó de l'Estelat; Tel. 972 36 48 00; Fax 972 37 16 37; category 1*

Santa Marta
Perfect for a relaxing stay; pretty location on the Santa Cristina bay. *76 rooms; closed 15 Dec–1 Feb; Tel. 972 364 9 04; Fax 972 36 9 2 80; category 1*

SPORTS & LEISURE

Motor sports
Go-carts: Carting Formula. *Carretera de Girona; Tel. 972 36 78 07*

Horse riding
Club Hípic: *Tel. 36 86 15;* Colorado: *Tel. 972 36 52 79;* Venta de Goya: *Tel. 972 36 45 38*

Fun at Marineland
Parc Aquátic – Water World: white-water course, swimming pool, slides, wave pool. *On the outskirts, towards Blanes, Carretera Vidreres, 1.2 km; Tel. 972 36 86 13; admission: 1,975 ptas, children under 1.45 m, 1,150 ptas*

Tennis
Sports centre next to the post office. *Tel. 972 36 66 13*

Water sports
Club Marítim Fenals. *Platja de Fenals; Tel. 972 36 63 71*
Club Nàutic Lloret. *Passeig de la Riera, s/n; Tel. 972 37 22 55*
Windsurfing Vent Blau. *Platja de Fenals; information at 972 36 52 00*

ENTERTAINMENT

Lloret has more than 50 discos, countless pubs and bars, as well as nightclubs and a casino (open till 4 am), the *Magic Park* (paradise for slot machine fans) and the *Gran Palace Lloret* (international cabaret with flamenco shows).

INFORMATION

Oficina d'Información Turística
Plaça de la Vila; Tel. 972 36 47 35; Fax 972 36 77 50; and at the bus terminal, Tel. 972 36 57 88; Fax 972 37 13 95; www.lloret.org

SURROUNDING AREA

Blanes   (108/B5-6)

At the southern end of the Costa Brava, Blanes (pop. 20,000) is an industrial town, specializing in textiles and fisheries, with a flourishing tourist industry. The beach, with its numerous hotels, is similar to that at Lloret. Here, though, the old town is still intact. After Lloret, Blanes is positively relaxing and offers a few unusual sights to boot. Take a look at the fishing port with its daily fish auctions and drop into one of the small fish restaurants round about.

To the north of the town, on a hill, are the ruins of an old fort, *Castell de Sant Joan*, which affords a breathtaking view across the town and along the coast. The 14th-century parish church of *Santa Maria* in the town centre has been completely renovated. In front of the church, Sardana groups dance in the evenings. The main attraction in Blanes is, however, the ★ *botanical garden – Jardí Botánic Mar i Murta (in summer:* daily, 9 am–6 pm; in winter Mon–Sat 10 am–5 pm, Sun 10 am–2 pm; admission: 200 ptas). German businessman Karl Faust began laying out the park in 1921. *Restaurant: Can Flores (Explanada del Port, s/n; Tel. 972 33 00 07; category 2),* which serves fish and seafood almost straight out of the net! *Information: Patronat Municipal de Turisme, Plaça de Catalunya, s/n; Tel. 972 33 03 48; Fax 972 33 46 86*

Just 20 km south of Blanes lies the village of Arenys de Mar **(111/D4)** and the ★ *Restaurant Hispania (closed Sun evenings, Tues, Holy Week and Oct; Carretera N II; Tel. 937 91 03 06; category 1–2),* which serves superb fish dishes. Don't forget to book a table!

Ermita Santa Cristina   (108/B5)

To the south of Lloret stands a small church, first mentioned in 1376, but completely rebuilt in the Baroque style at the end of the 18th century. The marble altar comes from Italy. Every year, Santa Cristina is the focal point

Fish auction, every day at 4 pm in Blanes

The legendary Ermita Santa Cristina – destination of the seaborne procession

of a picturesque procession of fishing boats off Lloret. Legend has it that the Italian martyr was executed in her homeland, her body pierced by several arrows and her corpse then thrown into the sea. Months later, fishermen from Lloret are said to have found her body, free of all signs of injury. The body was returned to Italy, except for a tooth, which is decorated with flowers and forms the centrepiece of the ceremony on the saint's day.

Sils (108/A3)

A small town of 1,800 souls, close to the motorway. Sils boasts an impressive *Motor Museum (daily, except Sun, 10 am–1 pm and 3 pm–6 pm; admission: 300 ptas; Tel. 972 85 30 20)*, a good idea, not just on rainy days. In 1950 businessman Salvador Claret began collecting fully functional old-timers. Today the collection numbers some 100 models, including a steam-driven Merry Weather, built in 1883, the oldest car in Spain that is still in running order.

PLATJA D'ARO

(109/E3) In summer, Platja d'Aro has 100,000 inhabitants, in winter there are just 5,000 left. That just about says it all. Is Platja d'Aro nothing more than a village? A summer-only city? A holiday factory! The most attractive thing here is the 3-km-long, golden beach. All along it, one hotel after the other has sprung up – part of the "who can build the most hotels in the shortest time?" competition, which was rife here in the 1960s. The town centre sits under a cloud of traffic-induced smog, the shops are expensive, so too are the bars and pubs (which cater mainly for German, English and Dutch tastes), and the discos are too loud. Even the sex trade, which drew so many visitors in the past, is not what it used to be, in an era overshadowed by Aids. What is it about Platja d'Aro which makes it so popular? Ninety-five thousand visitors can't be wrong, can they? Why don't you just go and see for yourself. You never know...

SIGHTS

Iglesia Parroquial de Platja d'Aro
The parish church – modern, of course, though in the style of a Catalan country house – stands in its own grounds, somewhat outside town and looks rather out of place. *Carrer de l'Església*

RESTAURANTS

Lots of them, mostly specializing in hamburgers and fish'n'chips. There are a few exceptions, though.

Aradi
Catalan cuisine, including fish. *Carretera Palamós; Tel. 972 81 73 76; category 2*

Carles Camós Big-Rock
Excellent fish menu and very good selection of wines. *Closed Sun*

The coast near Platja d'Aro, with many a hidden bathing spot

evenings and Mon; Barri de Fanals, 5; Tel. 972 81 80 12; category 1

L'Esquinade
Another good address for fish-lovers. *Pinar del mar, 13; Tel. 972 81 84 24; category 2*

Llevant
Plenty of fresh fish on the menu, and even the locals come here to eat. *Carretera de Palamós, 33; Tel. 972 81 75 37; category 2*

SHOPPING

Countless boutiques and shops selling cheap souvenirs. There are also a few good cake shops and grocery stores. Market day is Friday.

HOTELS

There's no shortage of hotels here, as you will have gathered. We have chosen a few hotels that can be recommended.

Carles Camós Big-Rock
The luxury hotel in Platja d'Aro. First-class restaurant (closed Sun evenings and Mon). *5 suites; closed Jan; Barri de Fanals, 5; Tel. 972 81 80 12; Fax 972 81 89 71; category 1*

Hostal de la Gavina
"The Seagull" is the best hotel on the Costa Brava. Luxury is just a way of life here, and, what's more, there is no air conditioning, so there's no danger of you catching a cold! *74 rooms; closed Nov–Holy Week; Plaça Rosaleda, s/n; in the neighbouring village of S'Agaró; Tel. 972 32 11 00; Fax 972 32 15 73; category 1*

Park Hotel San Jorge

Most pleasant hotel, since it lies outside town on the way to Palamós. Set in a bay, it also has tennis courts. *103 rooms; closed Dec–Feb; Condado San Jorge; Tel. 972 65 23 11; Fax 972 65 25 76; category 1*

Els Pins

Modest hotel with small restaurant. *65 rooms; closed Nov–end-March; Nostra Senyora del Carme, 34; Tel. 972 81 72 19; Fax 972 81 75 46; category 2*

SPORTS & LEISURE

By far the best thing going for Platja d'Aro is its beach. It is scrupulously well maintained. In the daytime, this is the place to be.

Amusement park

Aguapark – water slides, various pools, ideal for children. *On the road leading to Palamós, Carretera de Circunvalación; open 9 am–6 pm*

Golf

Club de Golf Costa Brava, 18 holes, guests welcome. *Santa Cristina d'Aro; Tel. 972 83 71 50*

Tennis

Club de Tenis d'Aro, *Paraje Gramoja, Castell d'Aro; Tel. 972 81 74 00*
Tennis-Squash-Platja, *Carrer Sant Feliu, 3; Tel. 972 81 70 06*

Water sports

Escola Municipal de Vela offers sailing and surfing. *Tel. 972 81 67 77*

ENTERTAINMENT

Second strong point in Platja d'Aro: the nightlife. There are all sorts of clubs, flamenco shows, pubs, Sangria bars, discotheques –

hearing deficiency and vision impairment included in the entrance price!

Club Náutico Port d'Aro

Skippers' Lounge. Relatively quiet club, situated at the marina. Meeting place for seafarers and both "nouveau and not-so-nouveau riche". The atmosphere is slightly more refined than amongst the paunches and shorts elsewhere! *Port d'Aro*

Kamel

⚡ Disco in a golden, pyramid-shaped building with two dance floors. *Carretera de Palamós, s/n*

Pacha

⚡ One of a chain of discos around Spain. It all began with the chic "Pacha" in Madrid. Now they're in Ibiza, Mallorca and other posh resorts. *Carretera Sant Feliu a Pinell*

INFORMATION

Foment Municipal de Turisme

Mossèn Jacinto Verdaguer, 4; Tel. 972 81 71 79; Fax 972 82 56 57

SURROUNDING AREA

Castell d'Aro   (109/E3)

Quiet, unspoilt village, 3 km west of Platja d'Aro. Ruins of a medieval castle.

S'Agaró   (109/E3)

This exclusive residential area between Platja d'Aro and Sant Feliu has been a sanctuary for the rich, the beautiful and the elderly since 1923. They live, hidden away in their villas, or in the *Hostal de la Gavina*, and dine at the *Taverna del Mar (Tel. 972 32 38 00; category 1)*, a nostalgic bathing establishment on the beach. Speciality of the house: excellent fish and seafood creations.

SANT FELIU DE GUÍXOLS

(**109/E3**) What a contrast to Platja d'Aro. Here, you'll find a splendid promenade, reminiscent of the French Riviera. The old town is intact and there are no multi-storey tourist shoe boxes. Consequently, the atmosphere in Sant Feliu de Guíxols is more agreeable and relaxed than elsewhere. No wonder the largest town on the coast (pop. 17,000) calls itself "the Queen of the Costa Brava". Sant Feliu has a long history: the Iberian king, Brigo, is said to have fallen in love with the bay and built a fortress here. Only many centuries later was it seized by the Moors, who were in turn dispossessed by Charlemagne. According to legend, the patron saint of the town, St Felix, drowned in the bay in AD 304. Today, Sant Feliu de Guíxols plays an important role, not only as an elegant holiday destination, but also as a cultural centre.

SIGHTS

Casa Patxot
Elegant town house on the Passeig del Mar, which today houses the regional Chamber of Commerce. The building is also home to an exhibition of cork products, celebrating an industry that has brought Sant Feliu de Guíxols prosperity and fame. *Passeig del Mar, 40*

Casino La Constancia
Villa decorated with towers, minarets and mosaics, giving it a very Arabic feel. Favourite meeting place for chess players. *Passeig des Gijols*

Ferrán Agullo monument
Stone monument on the *Sant Elm* mountain, dedicated to the poet Ferrán Agullo, who coined the phrase Costa Brava to describe this stretch of the Spanish coast.

Sant Feliu cemetery
Very interesting gravestones and monuments in the style of Catalan Art Nouveau. *On the outskirts of town, turn right off the road leading to Tossa*

Iglesia Sant Feliu
Fourteenth-century Romanesque-Gothic church, originally part of a monastery. *Plaça Monestir*

Plaça Monestir
Square featuring the remains of an old Benedictine monastery from the tenth century. Charlemagne is said to have adapted the Iberian royal castle that originally stood on the site and dedicated it to Saint Felix.

Porta Ferrada
Elegant arcade dating from the 11th century. Part of the remains of the monastery portico with Romanesque windows and a Baroque portal. *Plaça Monestir*

MUSEUM

Museu Municipal
Exhibition of archaeological finds, such as a Roman mosaic, and works of Catalan folk art. *Plaça Monestir; daily, 11 am–1 pm and 5 pm–8 pm (July/Aug), otherwise Sun 11 am–1 pm; free admission*

Like Roses, Sant Feliu is prized for its excellent restaurants, which are very popular amongst gourmet diners from Barcelona and Girona.

Bahia
The superb local specialities draw plenty of guests to this restaurant on the promenade, which also features a nightclub where flamenco is performed! *Passeig del Mar, 17; Tel. 972 32 02 19; category 2*

Can Toni
❖ The kitchen here has been turning out top-quality local fare for 75 years. Highly recommended by the locals! *Closed Tues and Oct–May; Garrofers, 54; Tel. 972 32 10 26; category 1–2*

Casa Buxo
Another long-running success story: 60 years of family-run, consistently high-quality regional cuisine. *Closed Oct–April; Carrer Major, 18; Tel. 972 32 01 87; category 1*

Eldorado Petit
Lluis Cruañas runs two restaurants, one in Barcelona, the other here in Sant Feliu. His speciality is Catalan cuisine with a French and an Italian touch. *Closed Wed and Nov; Rambla Vidal, 11; Tel. 972 32 18 18; category 1*

Montserrat – Can Salvi
One of the main attractions here is the lovely beach terrace, and naturally the menu highlight: fillet of sole with Roquefort. *Closed Wed and Jan–Feb; Passeig del Mar, 23; Tel. 972 32 10 13; category 2*

S'Adolitx
First-class fish restaurant. *Closed in winter; Carrer Major, 13; Tel. 972 32 18 53; category 2*

The streets of the pretty town centre and the promenade along the beach tempt the visitor to indulge in a lengthy shopping spree. Here, you'll find boutiques and souvenir shops, fine grocers and delicatessens, as well as dealers selling local crafts.

Every Sunday, the square in front of the Town Hall is the setting for the weekly market, with stands offering fresh fruit and vegetables, fish and products from local farms. Textiles, reasonably priced clothes and household items are also on sale.

Caleta Park
Attractive, sophisticated hotel on the Platja de Sant Pol, with tennis courts and a swimming

---

In the spirit of Marco Polo

Marco Polo was the first true world traveller. He travelled with peaceful intentions forging links between the East and the West. His aim was to discover the world, and explore different cultures and environments without changing or disrupting them. He is an excellent role model for the travellers of today and the future. Wherever we travel we should show respect for other peoples and the natural world.

pool. *105 rooms; closed Oct until Holy Week; Platja de Sant Pol, s/n, S'Agaró; Tel. 972 32 00 12; Fax 972 32 40 96; category 1*

Plaça

Comfortable hotel situated on the market place; no restaurant. *16 rooms; Plaça Mercat, 22; Tel. 972 32 51 55; Fax 972 82 13 21; category 2*

Rex

Small and modest, but nicely situated house. *25 rooms; closed Oct–May; Rambla del Portalet, 16; Tel. 972 82 18 09; category 2*

SPORTS & LEISURE

Leisure centre

Els Quatre Arbres, Parque de Atracciones. Horse riding, tennis, trampolines, miniature golf. *Carretera de Girona, s/n; Tel. 972 32 04 59*

Diving

Centre d'Activitats Subaquatiques. *Rutll, 41; Tel. 972 32 23 96;* Eden Roc Diving Center. *Carrer Punta de Garbi, 7; Tel. 972 32 53 87*

Tennis

Carrer Colón, s/n; Tel. 972 32 10 50

Water sports

Club Nàutic Sant Feliu (sailing, courses available). *Zona Esportiva del Port; Tel. 972 32 17 00* Escola de Windsurf. *Platja de Sant Pol; no Tel.*

ENTERTAINMENT

Sant Feliu provides a whole host of bars, pubs, discos and nightclubs along the ✻ Passeig del Mar and elsewhere in the town centre. The acclaimed Festival Internacional de Música is held in July.

INFORMATION

Oficina Municipal de Turisme
Plaça Monestir, 54; Tel. 972 82 00 51; Fax 972 82 01 19

SURROUNDING AREA

Ermita de Sant Elm　　(109/E3)
✲✲ Hermitage, situated in the hills above Sant Feliu and dedicated to Saint Telmus. It's certainly well worth taking the trouble to walk up here for the incredible view across the cork oak groves, the rocky coves along the deeply fissured coastline and the town of Sant Feliu.

Coast road
to Tossa de Mar　　(109/E3–D4)
★ ✲✲ If you're travelling by car, then take this route; it demonstrates admirably how this stretch of coastline earned its "wild" label. This is pure Costa Brava. Fabulous panoramic views.

Pedralta　　(109/D3)
✲✲ This famous natural monument, to the west of Sant Feliu in the direction of Girona, is the largest of its kind in Spain. The "tall stone" balances precariously on top of another and can be tipped backwards and forwards, without toppling down. Superb view over land and sea!

Santa Cristina d'Aro　　(109/D3)
Baroque parish church featuring a 17th-century retabel and standing in the idyllic Riu Ridaura valley, to the west of Sant Feliu. Close by is the golf club of the same name.

TOSSA DE MAR

(108–109/C–D4) This is the prettiest built-up area on the southern stretch of the Costa Brava. Tossa, with some 3,000 inhabitants, has an intact medieval old town, whose walls and towers can be seen for miles around. It lies in a beautiful bay, and the city fathers are breaking new ground in terms of local development.

Whereas local politicians in other villages have long been jealous of the lucrative tourist industry in Platja d'Aro or Lloret, the powers that be in Tossa could think of no worse fate for their town: revenue, yes, but at what cost? They decided to look to the high end of the market and cater for a more sophisticated clientele. A strange thought, maybe, when you look at the sheer numbers of visitors to the Costa Brava. Tossa was the first town on the Costa Brava to have a sewage clarification plant, which it followed up with a sea-water purification plant. Finally, they even banned bullfighting! Nowadays, environmental conferences take place here and the EU blue flag flies at the beach to testify to the quality of the water.

SIGHTS

Capilla de la Virgen del Socorro
Small chapel, built in 1593, standing in the middle of the town centre. *Carrer Mare de Deu del Socorro*

Iglesia de Sant Vicent
Tossa's 18th-century Baroque parish church. *(Fri 5.30 pm–6.30 pm); Carrer Església; free admission*

Seagull monument
Dedicated to the "genuine Juan Gaviota in us all". The sculpture represents a seagull in flight, a symbol of freedom, and a tribute to Richard Bach's bestseller, *Jonathan Livingston Seagull. Passeig del Mar*

Vila Romana
Remains of a Roman settlement, found in 1914. The mosaics are especially beautiful. *Av. del Pelegrí*

Vila Vella
★ The old town in Tossa is like a museum, peopled with live exhibits! It is enclosed by medieval fortifications dotted with numerous defensive towers and built in the 12th century to ward off pirate attacks. In the upper part stand the ruins of a Gothic church. This part has been lovingly restored and is held to be one of the most beautiful in Spain; a classic symbol of the Costa Brava. You'll also find plenty of restaurants here.

MUSEUMS

Casa de la Cultura
Temporary art exhibitions in the courtyard of the former San Miguel hospital. *Av. del Pelegrí, 8; daily, 4 pm–9 pm; free admission*

Museu Municipal
Fabulous collection of paintings on display in the former Governor's Palace, directly adjacent to the city wall of the Vila Vella. Works by such artists as Mercader, Sacharow and Chagall, who spent the summer of 1934 in Tossa and called it his "blue paradise". It was here that he painted the famous picture *The Heavenly Violinist*, which is also on show here: the flight of a violinist standing before an open Tossa

window, looking out onto a view of Chagall's birthplace, Vitebsk. Another exhibit of note is the section of mosaic from a fourth-century Roman villa. *Plaça Roig y Soler; daily, 10 am–1 pm and 4 pm–8 pm, Sun 11 am–1 pm; admission: 250 ptas*

Pinacoteca Municipal

Alternating art exhibitions during the summer months. *Carrer Victor Catalá, s/n; daily, 5 pm–8 pm; free admission*

Bahía

Famous restaurant on the promenade, attracting many regular diners. Noted for its fish, the speciality of the house is *Simitomba* (fish with potatoes). *Closed over Christmas; Passeig del Mar, 19; Tel. 972 34 03 22; category 1–2*

Can Joan Pescador

Modest establishment, next to the football pitch, serving good, down-to-earth food made from fresh ingredients. *Carrer Doctor Fleming, 2; Tel. 972 34 12 14; category 3*

Es Molí

Original restaurant in an old mill, with a large chimney and courtyard full of orange trees. The fish is a must, though the Catalan meat dishes are worth a try as well. *Closed Tues and mid-Dec–mid-Feb; Carrer Tarull, 5; Tel. 972 34 14 14; category 1–2*

Sa Palma

No frills restaurant, but if you like entrails or pasta with black squid sauce, this is the place for you. *Sant Raimont de Penyafort, 11; Tel. 972 34 20 51; category 2*

The Avinguda Costa Brava is lined with good shops.

Everest

The finest Lladró porcelain for the collector, at a pretty price. *Carrer Pola, 1*

Galería Art Tossa

Art gallery that sells paintings and sculptures by Catalan artists. *Carrer de la Virgen del Socorro, 12*

Medieval castle in the otherwise forward-looking Tossa de Mar

Magatzens Palou

Tossa's biggest shopping centre, packed with bric-a-brac, Spanish household items and everything you thought you ever needed, but didn't. *Carrer de Costa Brava*

Nasta

Selection of well-crafted, old silver jewellery in extensive showrooms. *Carrer Pou de la Vila, 11*

HOTELS

Canaima

Reasonably priced hotel. *17 rooms; closed Oct–end of May; Av. de la Palma, 24; Tel. 972 34 09 95; Fax 972 34 26 26; category 3*

Mar Menuda

Very attractive luxury hotel, situated directly on the beach, with swimming pool and beautiful terrace. *50 rooms; closed Nov–26 Dec; Playa de Mar Menuda, s/n; Tel. 972 34 10 00; Fax 972 34 00 87; category 1*

Reymar

Tossa de Mar's No. 1 luxury hotel. Tastefully furnished, it also offers a luxurious pool and tennis courts. The magnificent view across the bay is included in the price. *166 rooms; closed Nov–April; Playa de Mar Menuda; Tel. 972 34 03 12; Fax 972 34 15 04; category 1*

SPORTS & LEISURE

Tennis

Hostal La Huerta, *Av. de Catalunya, s/n; Tel. 972 34 02 21*

Water sports

Aristos Club, sailing, surfing, water-skiing and diving. *Camping Cala Llevado; Tel. 972 34 12 77*

ENTERTAINMENT

Owing to its idyllic appearance, Tossa de Mar is still an international tourist destination with the corresponding palette of night-time attractions. The cheapest way to spend an evening is to stroll down the Passeig del Mar and through the medieval town, past the Avinguda de Costa Brava or the Plaça de Espanya.

Catxa-Club

Posh open-air disco, with its own pool. A little way out of town. *Carretera Sant Feliu, approx. 1.2 km to the north*

Night Club Paradis

The fun starts down on the beach at 10 pm. *Passeig del Mar, 53; no Tel.*

Tortuga

Cosy bar with a pleasant view of the sea. *Sant Raimont de Penyafort, 13*

Vila Vella

Agreeable bar with terrace, right in the middle of Tossa, up on the hill. Don't overdo the punch–you have to negotiate the cobbled streets again when you leave! *Vila Vella*

INFORMATION

Oficina Municipal de Turisme

Carretera de Lloret (at the bus station); Tel. 972 34 01 08; Fax 972 34 07 12

SURROUNDING AREA

In the immediate vicinity of Tossa de Mar are numerous pretty coves, a veritable paradise for divers. One of the finest is *L'Infern en Caixa*, an intriguing gorge cutting deep into the coastline.

Fantastic bays and Surrealism

These routes are marked in green on the map on the inside front cover and in the Road Atlas beginning on page 100

① ON THE TRAIL OF SALVADOR DALI

The visitor who wants to increase his understanding of the works of Surrealist painter Salvador Dalí (1907–1989) should turn his attention to the Costa Brava in which Dalí spent the greater part of his life and where the majority of his works originated. The artist is inextricably linked with his homeland and, strange as it may seem, his pictures demonstrate a degree of harmony with the landscape of the northern Costa Brava. This route, then, takes us not only to the most notable cornerstones and places of pilgrimage of the "Surrealist triangle" – to Figueres, Cadaqués and Púbol – but also to the north coast that Dalí and his wife so loved, to the beaches, the old towns and villages, to the ruins of ancient civilizations and to typical restaurants. The 180-km round trip can be completed in a day, but in order to appreciate fully the spectacular surroundings, you should ideally allow yourself two or three days.

The trip begins in *Figueres (p. 52)* with a real highlight, a visit to the *Teatro Museo Dalí (p. 53)*. All that remains of the former municipal theatre is the clas-

sical façade. But before we go in, we're given a taste of the bizarre world of this great artist: a row of over-sized egg-shaped sculptures perches on the edge of the roof, and above the door hangs an old diving suit in which Dalí almost suffocated during a speech! The weird and wonderful collection also contains the famous *Rainy Taxi*. Pop a coin in the slot and watch as the dummy passengers and driver are drenched in a torrent of rain inside the car. Dalí was buried here in the museum, his inconspicuous resting place going unnoticed by most visitors.

The figure of Dalí permeates the town of Figueres through and through. He was born here, the son of a notary, and was christened after his elder brother, who died in childhood before Dalí was born – a fact that had a strong impact on his later life, for Dalí took his name to be a kind of omen. Other Dalí-relevant sights include the church of *Sant Pere*, where he was christened, and the *Castell de Sant Ferran*, where he did his military service.

Carry on along the coast on the main N 260 road to *Llançà (p. 41)*, which you reach in about half an hour. This pretty fishing village nestles in a delightful bay, affording a magnificent view out to sea and up into the mountains. A word about lunch: on the Costa Brava, you never sit down to eat before 1.30 pm. Try *Can Manuel (p. 41)* for its fine fish dishes.

Next stop: *El Port de la Selva (p. 42)*. This, too, is an idyllic fishing village in a bay, which almost closes in on itself, creating a lake-like calm. Take your siesta on the beach, which has been awarded a blue flag for the quality of the water. When the sun has lost some of its intensity, drive up towards the ruined monastery of *Sant Pere de Rodes (p. 43)*. The final 100 m or so have to be covered on foot, but it's an acceptable price to pay for what you get: the view is 100 per cent pure Costa Brava.

As the sun slowly sets, drive the last 12 km through the rugged mountain landscape to *Cadaqués (p. 36)*, next point on the "Surrealist triangle". Dalí spent the summer holidays of his childhood in this town so rich in character, and later attributed to it a certain "magical imponderability". The *Museo Municipal de Arte Contemporáneo* and the *Museo Perrot Moore (p. 37)* contain works by Dalí. Stay the night in nearby *Port Lligat*, birthplace of Dalí's father *(p. 41)*, in the *Hotel Port Lligat (p. 39)*, and take your evening meal in one of Cadaqués's many restaurants. Follow this up with a stroll along the promenade and then – exhausted, probably – call it a day with a night cap at *La Habana* bar *(p. 39)* or at *L'Hostal (p. 39)*.

Next morning, admire the view from the hotel terrace over to a small bay and its fishing boats – and across to the eggs on the roof of the building next door. This time its the former fisherman's cottage, converted and extended by Dalí over the years to create the unconventional residence we see today. Now a *museum (p. 41)*, it gives a vivid insight into the lifestyle of the artist and his wife Gala. Before leaving Port Lligat, make a short detour to the untamed cliff landscape of *Cap de Creus (p. 40)*, the easternmost tip of Spain.

The next 15 km, along a narrow mountain road, take you to quiet *Cala Montjoi* – not that far when you consider that true gourmets come from miles around to get here. Their destination, the restaurant *Hacienda El Bulli (p. 57)*, run by master chef Ferrán Adrià, is one of the finest in Spain. The next stage of the journey ends in the little town of *Roses (p. 56)*, which – apart from its long beach and promenade, interesting fishing port and overgrown ancient Greek settlement – has little in the way of major attractions.

Further on, in *Castelló d'Empúries*, take a look at the impressive *Gothic cathedral of Santa Maria (p. 59)*. The route now turns south, towards Sant Pere Pescador and crosses – in summer – the shimmering plain that Dalí called "the most concrete and objective landscape in the world". His tribute to this landscape is the world-famous picture *The Persistence of Memory*, showing pocket watches melting in the heat. Along the coast is also the *Parc Natural dels Aiguamolls de l'Empordà (p. 59)*, one of the largest areas of wetland habitat in the Mediterranean region and the breeding grounds of many species of waterfowl.

From here it is just a few kilometres to another Costa Brava highlight, the ruins of *Empúries (p. 49)*, the largest Greco-Roman city in Spain, which was founded in the sixth century BC. A walk around the site takes between one and two hours. Close the second stage of this tour with a dip in the sea and a sunbathe at one of the clean beaches at *L'Escala (p. 47)*. This is also a good place to eat in the evening and stay the night, for example, at the *Nieves Mar (p. 49)*.

The third day begins with the journey to historical *Torroella de Montgrí (p. 61)* and its satellite town *L'Estartit (p. 61)*. The latter is a tourist centre that is overrun in summer, but then again it does have one of the longest and most beautiful beaches on the Costa Brava. We recommend an outing to the nature reserve of the *Medes Islands (p. 66)* in a so-called "aquarium boat". You can observe the underwater flora and fauna through the glass-panelled hull; a diver's paradise, too. A tip for night owls: the tourist scene in L'Estartit.

Back to Torroella de Montgrí now, then on along the C 255 towards Girona. Turn off at Serra de Daró for a look at the *Ciutat iberica d'Ullastret (p. 67)*, an ancient Iberian settlement, dating from the sixth century BC.

Continuing along the C 255, take the turn-off near La Pera to *Púbol*. This is the final point on the Dalí triangle: *Púbol Castle (15 March–Oct: daily, except Mon, 10.30 am–5.30 pm; 15 June–15 Sept: daily until 7.30 pm)*. Dalí gave the castle to his wife, Gala, as a present. Following her death in Port Lligat in 1982, Dalí had her body transported on the back seat of a Cadillac to Púbol Castle, where she was buried in the crypt. The car stands in an outbuilding on the estate, the key still in the ignition. Dalí stayed on here in the palace for some time, but following a fire in which he was seriously injured, he moved back to Figueres. The museum here is a dramatic statement on the life and times of the diva and her eccentric husband, who left his mark on the property in the form of the long-legged elephants, for example, in the garden.

To round off this tour, another highlight: a stroll through the streets of *Girona (p. 68)*, with its numerous historical sites, such as the *old town, the old university building, the cathedral, the Arabian Baths* and *the Jewish Quarter*. If you enjoy Catalan food, you'll find many good restaurants, such as the *Albereda (p. 70)*. It's just a 30-km drive back to Figueres.

② ALONG THE WILD COAST

This tour takes you to the best known spots in the region, through breathtaking countryside and past picturesque coves. You have to take the rough with the smooth, though, and the pretty side of the itinerary is balanced against the sins of the tourist planners – a seemingly endless chain of concrete eyesores to accommodate the masses. But this, too, is part of the Costa Brava. Fortunately, several villages and towns have chosen to preserve what remains of their original character. The whole tour takes one day, though you could just as easily take your time to enjoy it. Round trip: approx. 100 km.

The tour gets under way in *Torroella de Montgrí (p. 61)*, which you leave in the direction of Begur, to the south. A few kilometres on, you reach the first stop, *Pals (p. 67)*, the prettiest town on the Costa Brava, a medieval village with the feel of a living museum about it. Make a short detour to *Punta* on the *Platja de Pals (p. 67)*: and treat yourself to lunch at *Sa Punta*, one of the best fish restaurants on the coast. After that, it's only a few minutes' journey to *Begur (p. 65)*, a small medieval town, whose Catalan flair makes it one of the finest on the Costa Brava.

Heading south, the coast road passes heavenly bays and first-class hotels, the *Aiguablava* or the *Parador Aiguablava (p. 66)*, for example, both offering amazing views of the sea and the coast. The road continues through the fishing villages of *Tamariu, Llafranc* and *Calella de Palafrugell (p. 73)*, before finally reaching the small, industrial town of *Palafrugell (p. 73)*, where you can visit the historical town centre, the Moorish city walls and experience the characteristic market, which is held every Sunday morning.

Our next destination, further to the south, is the port of *Palamós (p. 71)*, with its important fishing harbour. The old town has remained intact, despite the demands of a growing tourist industry. The fabulous views that accompany you on your way down the coast road go some way to compensating for the sight of the high-rise tourist bunkers that scar such spots as *Platja d'Aro (p. 80)*. Here, things really start heating up for young holidaymakers when the sun has gone down. An oasis in the "disco desert" is the *Hostal de la Gavina (p. 81)*, a truly luxurious hotel.

Sant Feliu de Guíxols (p. 83), the next stop on the tour, is a pleasant contrast to Platja d'Aro. The town prides itself on being the "Queen of the Costa Brava" – not too great an exaggeration, either, thanks to its bright and cheerful atmosphere, smart promenade (shades of the Riviera!) and an authentic old town, ideal for a stroll. The picture is similar in *Tossa de Mar (p. 86)*, which you come to at the end of the prettiest stretch of coast road. You are presented with an unforgettable scene; the medieval town perched on a hill over the bay and the newer districts. Despite the hustle and bustle amongst the crowds of tourists, you'll feel at home in the narrow streets and on the well-tended beach. In addition, Tossa de Mar boasts several good restaurants, hotels and the nightlife to match.

South of Tossa begins that stretch of the Costa Brava that those with an eye for beauty judge to be a nightmare, but that attracts young people with small bank accounts. You arrive in *Lloret de Mar (p. 76)*, capital of mass tourism: a fabulous beach, lined with endless hotel façades. The town, with its almost 100,000 residents, could be renamed "Disco City", in recognition of Lloret's ability to party all night long! A tiny speck of light on the cultural horizon is the white church, *Ermita Santa Cristina (p. 79)*, focal point of an annual fishermen's procession.

Last stop on the journey is *Blanes (p. 79)*, an industrial town with some touristic appeal. It is worth visiting mainly because of the *fishing port* with its daily fish auction and for its main attraction, the Botanical Garden, the *Jardí Botánic Mar i Murta (p. 79)*.

From Blanes to *Barcelona (p. 30)*, it's a mere 60 km – the fascinating Catalan capital is a sight too good to miss.

Practical information

Important addresses and useful information for your visit to the Costa Brava

AMERICAN & BRITISH ENGLISH

Marco Polo travel guides are written in British English. In North America certain terms and usages deviate from British usage. Some of the more frequently encountered examples are (American given first):

baggage = luggage; cab = taxi; car rental = car hire; drugstore = chemist; fall = autumn; first floor = ground floor; freeway/highway = motorway; gas(oline) = petrol; railroad = railway; restroom = toilet/lavatory; streetcar = tram; subway = underground/tube; toll-free numbers = freephone numbers; trailer = caravan; trunk = boot (of a car); vacation = holiday; wait staff = waiter/waitress; zip code = post code.

BANKS

Opening times: generally Mon–Fri, 9 am–2 pm, Sat 9 am–12.30 pm (not all branches). Eurocheques are seldom accepted, but there are numerous automatic cash dispensers available. Foreign exchange bureaux can be found in larger towns and are also open in the afternoon. Many restaurants, hotels and shops accept credit cards, most commonly Visa.

CAMPING

There are some 300 (official) camp sites, divided into four categories: luxury, first, second and third class. They all offer satisfactory sanitary facilities and often have a swimming pool and tennis courts. The camping guide "Guía Campings" is available free of charge from most local tourist information offices. A complete list of all camp sites can be obtained from the Spanish Tourist Offices.

CHILDREN

Between the exuberant nightlife on the one hand and the many cultural highlights on the other, the Costa Brava is also an ideal choice for a family holiday. It is typical of the southern European mentality to involve children in all aspects of the holiday, be it in restaurants, at concerts, even in the disco! Many beaches have children's play areas and the larger hotels offer day nurseries or entertainment programmes for children. The police and pharmacies have details of the nearest paediatrician. Families with very small children are advised not to travel in July or August, since the weather is too hot.

CLIMATE

From June to September it can get very hot on the Costa Brava, with temperatures exceeding 30°C (86°F). In the evening, though and at night, temperatures can drop quite substantially. In April, May, October and November, don't forget to pack your umbrella for your trip to the Costa Brava. Otherwise, the climate in Catalonia is mild.

CUSTOMS

Inside the EU, there are no limits of goods for personal use. Outside the EU, goods can be carried between countries within the following limits: 200 cigarettes or 50 cigars or 250 g of tobacco; 1 l of spirits; 2 l of wine; 250 ml of eau de toliette and 50 g of perfume.

DRIVING

Speed limits: in built-up areas: 50 km/h; on secondary roads: 90 km/h; on highways: 120 km/h. The legal limit is 50 mg alcohol/100 ml of blood. It is recommended you bring a green insurance card with you and take out international travel insurance and fully comprehensive insurance policies. There is a good network of filling stations selling lead-free gas *(sin plomo)*. In the event of an accident, make sure you have two (preferably Spanish) witnesses, and notify your own third party insurer and its Spanish agency. Do not sign any admission of guilt! In the case of minor accidents, come to an agreement with the other party, who is likely to be under-insured – it saves a lot of trouble later. If major damage occurs, or if someone is injured, you must notify the police. Cars can be rented for around 8,589 ptas per day (small models).

EMBASSIES

British Embassy
Calle de Fernando el Santo, 16, 28010 Madrid; Tel. 91 700 82 00; Fax 91 700 82 72

Embassy of the United States of America
Serrano, 75, 28006 Madrid; Tel. 91 587 22 00; Fax 91 587 23 03

Canadian Embassy
Edificio Goya, Calle Nunez de Balboa, 35, 28001 Madrid; Tel. 91 423 32 50; Fax 91 4233251.

EMERGENCIES

Urgencia – the emergency telephone number for the police is valid for the whole of Spain: *091 (Policía Nacional, national) or 092 (Policía Municipal, local). In the event of a traffic accident, also 352 61 61.*

HEALTH

In large resorts, there are *centros médicos* with multi-lingual staff. On-the-spot first aid is available on many beaches at the Red Cross centres. For minor ailments, consult the *practicantes* at the nearest *casa de socorro*. The next police station *(emergency telephone number: 091)* can tell you where the next doctor *(médico)* can be contacted. Holiday guests are strongly advised to take out additional health insurance for the duration of their stay.

INFORMATION

Spanish Tourist Office
In Great Britain: *22–23 Manchester Square, London W1M 5AP; Tel. 020/74 86 80 77; Fax 020/74 86 80 34*
In the United States: *666 Fifth Avenue, 35th Floor, New York, NY 10103; Tel. 212/265 88 22; Fax 212/265 88 64; e-mail: oetny@ tourspain.es*
In Canada: *2 Bloor Street West, 34th Floor, Suite 3402, Toronto, Ontario M4W 3E2; Tel. 416/961 31 31; Fax 416/961 19 92; e-mail: toronto @tourspain.es*

MEASURES & WEIGHTS

1 cm	0.39 inches
1 m	1.09 yards (3.28 feet)
1 km	0.62 miles
1 m²	1.20 sq. yards
1 ha	2.47 acres
1 km²	0.39 sq. miles
1 g	0.035 ounces
1 kg	2.21 pounds
1 British ton	1016 kg
1 US ton	907 kg

1 litre is equivalent to 0.22 Imperial gallons and 0.26 US gallons

NEWSPAPERS

In the larger tourist centres on the Costa Brava, the major newspapers are often available in the evening on the day of going to press. Visitors who can read Spanish should choose *El País*, the leading national daily in Spain.

NUDISM

Going topless is no problem wherever you are in Spain, provided you keep it to the beach. Women who go shopping topless in the supermarket, for example, are no longer just laughed at, but rather pitied or even scorned. Bathing in the nude is quite another matter. You can swim and sunbathe in secluded coves, but there are only two official nudist camps on the Costa Brava: Relax-Nat in Mont Ras near Girona and El Toro Bravo in Viladecanx near Barcelona. For further information, contact: *Federación Española Naturismo (FEN), Mallorca 221, 3, 2 a, 08 008 Barcelona.*

PASSPORT & VISA

Within the EU, private individuals are no longer subject to customs checks; citizens of EU countries, the USA and Canada require an identity card or valid passport to enter the country. Children under 16 require either a children's passport or their names must be entered in the passport of a parent.

PETS

Dogs and cats require a certificate of health from a veterinary medical officer and proof of vaccination against rabies. This must have occurred at least 30 days, but not longer than one year, prior to entry.

POST & TELEPHONES

Post offices *(Correos y Telégrafos)* are generally open as follows:

Mon–Fri, 9 am–1 pm and 4 pm–6 pm, Sat 9 am–1 pm. Stamps *(sellos)* can also be bought at tobacconist's *(estancos)*. The post boxes are bright yellow. It is possible to send a telegram from Spanish post offices, but not to make a phone call.

It is possible to make direct telephone calls abroad from many public telephones, in some cases using 25- or 100-ptas coins, otherwise with telephone cards worth from 1,000 ptas. These *tarjetas telefónicas* are available at tobacconist's and some newsagents.

In addition, larger towns also have so-called telephone containers, where you pay for your call on leaving the booth. After 10 pm, international calls are around 25 % cheaper. To make an international call, dial 00, await the dialling tone, then dial the country code: 44 for the UK and 1 for the USA and Canada. Then dial the area code (without the zero) and the subscriber number required. The country code for Spain is 0034. Within Spain, there are no longer separate area codes; these are now part of the individual subscriber's number.

International phone calls can be made from public telephone booths, without any problems

PUBLIC TRANSPORT

There are good links between the larger towns on the Costa Brava and to Barcelona. The largest (private) bus company is called *Sarfa*. Rail connections are particularly good between towns on the southern Costa Brava and Barcelona. The tracks generally run parallel to the beach. Good connections between Barcelona and Girona. For more information, ask at the local station (Renfe).

TAXIS

Taxis are free if a sign saying *libre* or a green light is displayed. Ask the driver about the fare before setting off, even if the taxi is equipped with a meter. Spanish taxi drivers charge numerous surcharges, such as for journeys to the theatre, airport, station or if carrying luggage. For long-distance journeys, the driver may charge for his return trip. A tip of around 10 per cent is acceptable. In case of difficulty, note down the licence number and report the incident to the next tourist information office.

TIPPING

If you were satisfied with the service in a restaurant or hotel, with the usher at the cinema or theatre, with the taxi driver or tour guide, a tip of between 5 % and 10 % is considered acceptable.

VOLTAGE

Voltage is 220 volts AC. For electrical appliances with a safety plug, use an adapter.

YOUTH HOSTELS

There are three youth hostels on the Costa Brava; Cerveri de Gi-rona Youth Hostel *(Dels Ciutadans 9; Tel. 972 21 81 21)*, in an old town house; Tramuntana Youth Hostel in Figueres *(Anicet de Pàges 2; Tel. 972 50 12 13)*, set in a park; L'Escala Youth Hostel *(Les Coves 11; Tel. 972 77 12 00)*, a country house situated between the beach and ancient ruins. You need a youth hostel identity card to stay here.

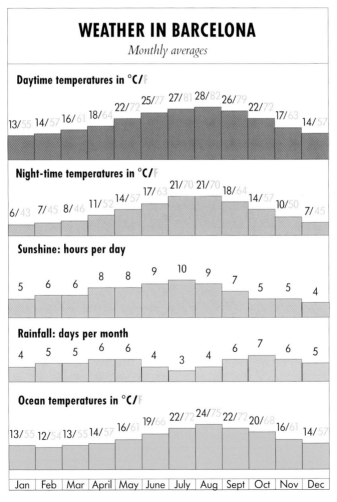

WEATHER IN BARCELONA
Monthly averages

Daytime temperatures in °C/F

13/55 14/57 16/61 18/64 22/72 25/77 27/81 28/82 26/79 22/72 17/63 14/57

Night-time temperatures in °C/F

6/43 7/45 8/46 11/52 14/57 17/63 21/70 21/70 18/64 14/57 10/50 7/45

Sunshine: hours per day

5 6 6 8 8 9 10 9 7 5 5 4

Rainfall: days per month

4 5 5 6 6 4 3 4 6 7 6 5

Ocean temperatures in °C/F

13/55 12/54 13/55 14/57 16/61 19/66 22/72 24/75 22/72 20/68 16/61 14/57

| Jan | Feb | Mar | April | May | June | July | Aug | Sept | Oct | Nov | Dec |

Do's and don'ts

Useful tips and advice on how to avoid some of the traps and pitfalls that await the unwary traveller

Don't reveal too much
Shorts, topless – that's OK – on the beach. And only there. (It's certainly alright to wear shorts on a long car journey, though!) When visiting restaurants, museums or churches, you should dress accordingly and not for an afternoon on the beach at Lloret. Your Spanish hosts will otherwise be rather amused, or in some cases even offended.

Don't get ripped off
You should be on your guard in the major tourist centres and, in particular, in Barcelona. Don't get involved in any betting or gaming on the streets, or buy anything from hawkers. Even if you feel confident about your command of Spanish, there are many cunning tricksters about who will always get the better of unwary tourists.

Don't park illegally
Take care to park your vehicle only in authorized car parks and parking spaces. The police do not beat about the bush and are quick to have offending vehicles towed away. It may not cost as much as at home, but it's twice as annoying. Besides, you are better off using public transport in Barcelona.

Don't drive too fast
Don't be tempted to drive like the locals, especially on the narrow, winding coast and mountain roads. They at least know their way around. Needless to say, they take far too many risks!

Don't go Dutch
Catalonia is a very hospitable region, and no self-respecting Catalan would dream of asking for separate bills in a restaurant. Pay for everything together – you can still split the costs later. This is one rule you really should abide by.

Don't forget your table manners
Do not, under any circumstances, sit down at a table that is already occupied. This is considered extremely rude, even if no offence is intended.

There is no shortage of alcohol on offer on the Costa Brava, and it tastes good, too. Wine with your fish, cognac with your coffee, an aperitif at the bar. Please remember one thing: the Catalan enjoys a drink as much as the next man, but he despises those who don't know when enough is enough.

On a positive note, it is perfectly acceptable to use your fingers when eating lobster and other shellfish.

Road Atlas of the Costa Brava

*Please refer to back cover for an overview
of this Road Atlas*

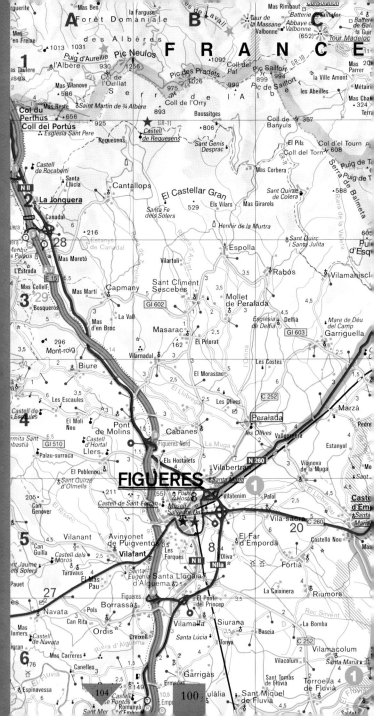

Cap Oullestrell
•125 Cap Castell
D
E
F

Côte Vermeille ★

Banyuls-sur-Mer
43• Cap l'Abeille
la Rhétorie
Puig
d'el Mas
•180
Col de Séris
Cap Rederis
Cap Peyrefite

Réserve Naturelle
Marine

1

Anse de Terrambou

505•
Mas de Mingou
Cerbère
Cap Cerbère

•207
Il dels Belitres
Col des Balistres

Portbou
(30)
Cala de las Ratas

Cap Marcer

MAR

N 260

Colera
Cap Llardó

MEDITERRÀNIA

2

linàs

el de Molinàs

67

Garbet
Badia de Cap Ras
Cap Ras

Grifeu
Hostal Grifeu
Badia Llançà

Isla Castella
El Port de Llançà

Setcases

Llançà

•197
La Valleta

4,5

Punta s'Arenella

Cap Gros

3

•327

5
430

168
El Port
de la Selva ★
El Golfet
la Galera

Punta dels Farallons
△ 95

Isla de Portaló
Illa de Cullaró
S'Encalladora

de
có

8

La Vall
de Santa Creu

2

Puig
de Cala Sardina

juïga

Dolmen del Mas
de la Mata

2,5

Sant Pere
de Rodes

La Selva
de Mar

Sant Baldiri

243

•62

Cap de
Creus ★

Pau

El Mas Isaac

Castell de
Sant Salvador

Serra de Rodes

Puig Alt Gran

Cala Bona

Punta d'en Codera

Palau-saverdera

Ermita
de Sant
Onofre

Perafita

4,5

Portlligat

Cala Portlligat
Illa de Portlligat

4

Vilaüt

GI 610

El Mas Fumats

Castell de
Bufalaranya

433

GI 614

Punta de
s'Oliguera

3,5

El Mas
Bosca

Cadaqués (23)

S'Arenella

La Garriga

El Mas Mates

2

El Mas Oliva

•463

El Pení
805•

Sant Sebastià

Badia de Cadaqués

Gruta

el Masnou
S

Santa
Margarida

Santa Maria
La Citadella

Roses

Cala Nans
Punta de sa Figuera

Platja Sta
Margarida

Puig Rom
225•

Montjoi

Mas
Chalet

Far de
Roses

Castell de la
Poncella

Torre de los
Sastres

Cala Montjoi

Cap de Norfeu ★
Cavall Bernat

5

Empuriabrava

Parc

Badia de Roses

Platja de
Canyelles Petites

Platja de
Canyelles Grosses

Cap Trencat
Punta Falconera

Cala Murtra

Natural

Platja de
Can Comes

Golf

Aiguamolls

de l'Empordà

de

3 km

6

Pere
ador

Mas Sopes

Platja de Sant
Pere Pescador

Llona
entera

Roses

101

105

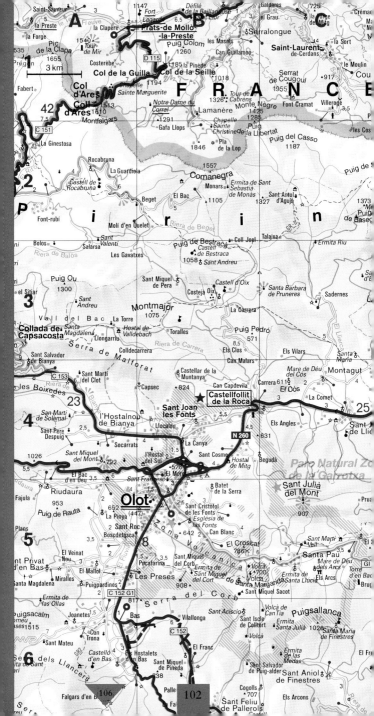

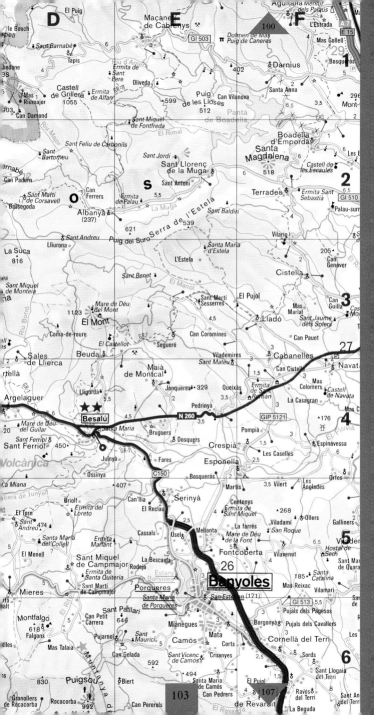

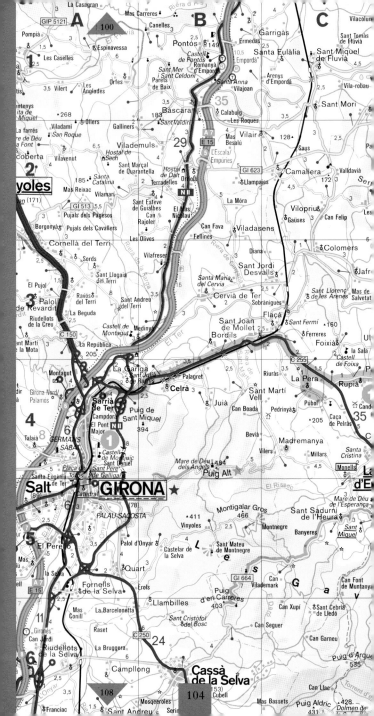

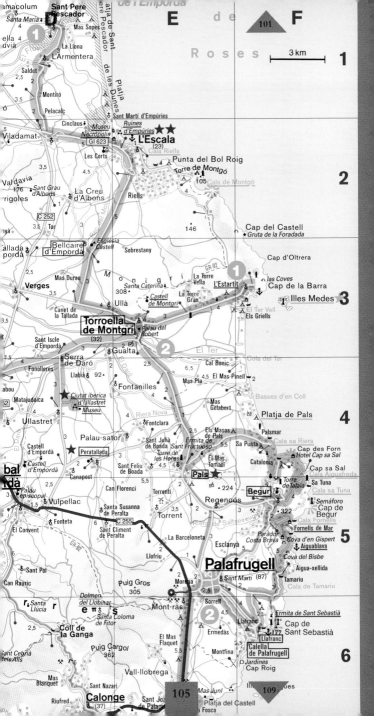

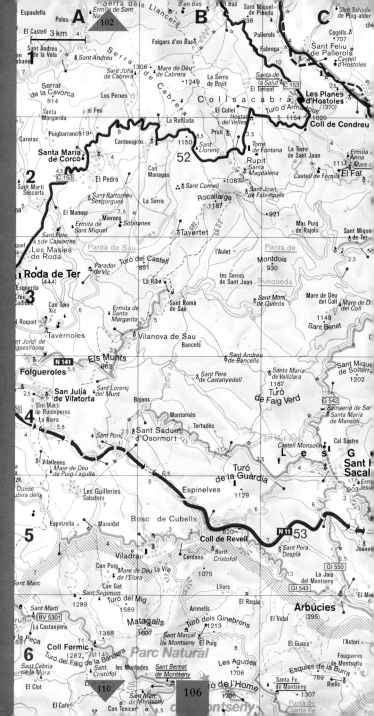

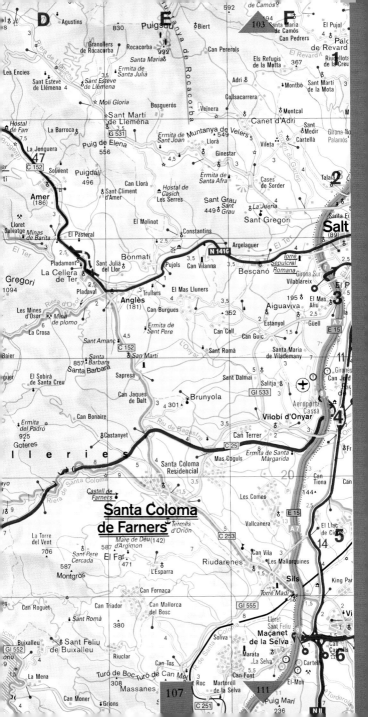

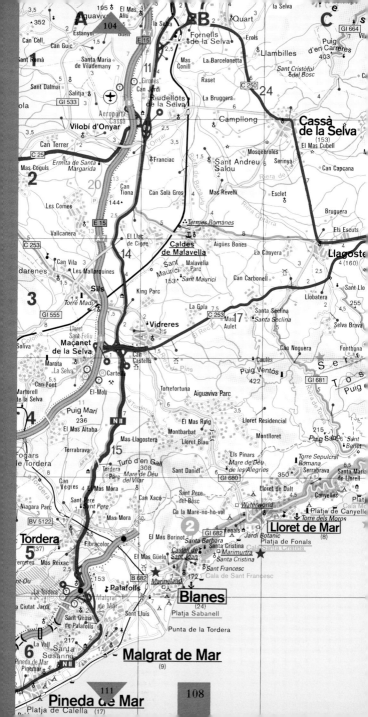

D **E** **F** Palafrug

Llofriu
105

Can Font
de Muntanya
Can Rauric
Sant Pol
Puig Gros
305
Sant Martí
Morella
Mont-ràs
Sorrell
2,5
Santa
Llúcia
Sant Cebrià
de Lledó
Dolmen
del Llobihar
Santa Coloma
de Fitor
e π š
Ermedàs
4,5

Can Garneu
El Mas
Flaquet
Montfina
2,5
Puig d'Arques
535
Sant Cebrià
dels Alls
Puig Cargol
362

Vall-llobrega

Can Llac
Mas
Blanquet
Sant Nazari
Mas Junl
uig Aldric
428
431
Dolmen de
la Cova d'en Daina
Riufred
Calonge
(37)
Sant Joan
de Palamós
Platja del Castell
Cala s'Alguer
Platja de la Fosca
d'Aro
Cabanyes
Sant Antoni
de Calonge
Santa Maria
74 Cap Gros
6,5
3,5
3,5
Romanyà
de la Selva
El Mas
Vila
Palamós
(14)
414
El Mas Ros
Torre Valentina
Platja de Roig
27
Bell-llac
Ampélit
La Roca
de Malvet
El Masnou
El Mas Vila
Les Teules
C 250
La Grota
Hotel Sant Jordi
Santa Maria
de Solias
Sta. Cristina
d'Aro
Castell
d'Aro
Platja d'Aro
Solius
Platja d'Aro
El Vilar
Torre
El Rome
Punta Prima
Cala de sa Conca
Sant Josep
Bufaganyes
Mas Trempat
s'Agaró ★★
Montclar
417
Pedralta
Platja Sant Pol
Sant Amanç
Puig de Cols
Sant Telm
Sant Pol
SANT FELIU DE GUIXOLS
Menhir
del Terma Gros
GI 682
Sant Elm
aldiri
13
Punta Brava
(4)
S'Estufador de Garbí

Sant Grau
Canyet
Punta del Romeguer
Platja de Canyet

Cala de Salionç
Salionç

Cap Pentiner
Cala de Giverola
Cala Pola
Cala Bona

Tossa de Mar ★★
(60)
Vila Vella
de Tossa
Boquera

MAR

MEDITERRÀNIA

3 km

1
2
3
4
5
6

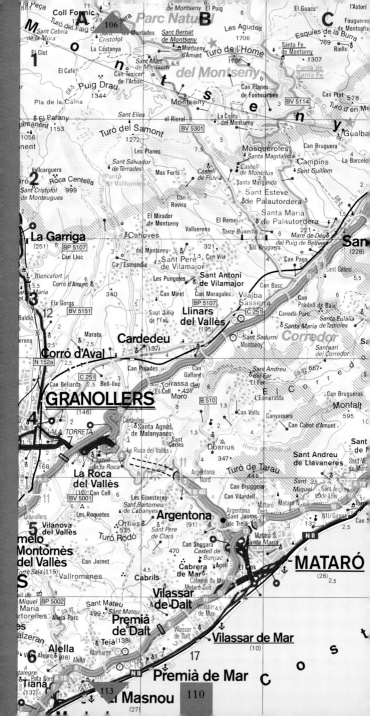

Palau
amans
Lliçà de Vall
199
Can Riera
Parets
del Vallès
El Carrer
de Baix
19
Circuit
de Catalunya
La Roca
del Vallès
Castell
de la
Les Coll
BV 5001
Les Ginesteres
Sant Bartomeu
de Cabanyes
Argentona
(91)
110

Palau
amans
ena
59
Poligon
Industrial
Gallecs
4,5 Mollet
L'Eixample
Parets
Vic
Granollers
Vilanova
del Vallès
Les Roquetes
Orrius
535
Sant Pere
de Clarà
Turó Rodó
Can Seg
Cas

Sta. Perpetua
ogoda
E 15
Montmelo
(81)
Montornès
del Vallès
Can Jornet
Vallromanes
Cabrils
470
Cabrera
de Mar
Cabre

à
es
Llagosta
Valles
Mollet
MOLLET
DEL VALLÈS
65
Martorelles
Castell de
Sant Miquel
BP 5002
Sant Maria
de Martorelles
Alella Parc
Sant Mateu
499 Sant Mateu
Premià
de Dalt
Vilassar
de Dalt
9

OLLET
Sant Fost
de Campsentelles
Can Boc
Turó de Galzeran
Vista Alegre
Alella
(88)
Teià(138)
Vilassar
de Dalt
2
17

Llagosta
78
Reixac
Sant Cebrià
de Cabanyes
La Correria
Montcada
14
485
Mare de Déu
de l'Alegria
Alella

466
Cartoixa de Montalegre
La Vallençana
El Mas Ram
Tiana
(132)
A 19
N II
Premià
(9)

Montcada
Torre de la Frares
303
Sant Crist
San Jerónimo
1,5
El Masnou
(27)

SINCUERUN
Montbau
B 20
Montgat

RIDIANA
LA TRINITAT
11
Turinat
56
Calvo Sotelo
STA. COLOMA
DE GRAMENET
3

CARMEL
HORTA
T. ANDREU
DE PALOMAR
Gran Via
Vemeda
Avda Alfonso XII
Bach de
Roda
Badalona
BADALONA
(24)
SANT ADRIÀ
DE BESÒS
St. Adrià de Besòs
Besòs

da
Familia
ACIA
Catedral
3.5 Plaça
Catalunya
Farò
POBLENOU
Poblenou
23
B 10
Museu Stra. Maria del Mar
Marítim Maremagnum
Torre San Sebastián
RACE
BARCELONA
(9)
★★
Genova 17h
4

IES
Palau
Nacional
19
Ciutat Vella
Port Mercaderies

stell
Montjuïc
PITALET DE LLOBREGAT
(4)
Zona
Franca
5

EGAT
M E D I T E R R À N I A
MAR
3 km
6

Eivissa 10 h
Palma de Mallorca 8 h
113
Maó (Menorca) 9 h

ROAD ATLAS LEGEND

Autobahn · Gebührenpflichtige Anschlussstelle · Gebührenstelle · Anschlussstelle mit Nummer · Rasthaus mit Übernachtung · Raststätte · Erfrischungsstelle · Tankstelle · Parkplatz mit und ohne WC		Motorway · Toll junction · Toll station · Junction with number · Motel · Restaurant · Snackbar · Filling-station · Parking place with and without WC
Autobahn in Bau und geplant mit Datum der Verkehrsübergabe		Motorway under construction and projected with completion date
Zweibahnige Straße (4-spurig)		Dual carriageway (4 lanes)
Fernverkehrsstraße · Straßennummern		Trunk road · Road numbers
Wichtige Hauptstraße		Important main road
Hauptstraße · Tunnel · Brücke		Main road · Tunnel · Bridge
Nebenstraßen		Minor roads
Fahrweg · Fußweg		Track · Footpath
Wanderweg (Auswahl)		Tourist footpath (selection)
Eisenbahn mit Fernverkehr		Main line railway
Zahnradbahn, Standseilbahn		Rack-railway, funicular
Kabinenschwebebahn · Sessellift		Aerial cableway · Chair-lift
Autofähre		Car ferry
Personenfähre		Passenger ferry
Schifffahrtslinie		Shipping route

Naturschutzgebiet · Sperrgebiet		Nature reserve · Prohibited area
Nationalpark, Naturpark · Wald		National park, natural park · Forest
Straße für Kfz. gesperrt		Road closed to motor vehicles
Straße mit Gebühr		Toll road
Straße mit Wintersperre		Road closed in winter
Straße für Wohnanhänger gesperrt bzw. nicht empfehlenswert		Road closed or not recommended for caravans
Touristenstraße · Pass	Weinstraße ⌃1510	Tourist route · Pass
Schöner Ausblick · Rundblick · Landschaftlich bes. schöne Strecke		Scenic view · Panoramic view · Route with beautiful scenery

Golfplatz · Schwimmbad		Golf-course · Swimming pool
Ferienzeltplatz · Zeltplatz		Holiday camp · Transit camp
Jugendherberge · Sprungschanze		Youth hostel · Ski jump
Kirche im Ort, freistehend · Kapelle		Church · Chapel
Kloster · Klosterruine		Monastery · Monastery ruin
Schloss, Burg · Schloss-, Burgruine		Palace, castle · Ruin
Turm · Funk-, Fernsehturm		Tower · Radio-, TV-tower
Leuchtturm · Kraftwerk		Lighthouse · Power station
Wasserfall · Schleuse		Waterfall · Lock
Bauwerk · Marktplatz, Areal		Important building · Market place, area
Ausgrabungs- u. Ruinenstätte · Feldkreuz		Arch. excavation, ruins · Calvary
Dolmen · Menhir		Dolmen · Menhir
Hünen-, Hügelgrab · Soldatenfriedhof		Cairn · Military cemetery
Hotel, Gasthaus, Berghütte · Höhle		Hotel, inn, refuge · Cave

Kultur / Culture

Malerisches Ortsbild · Ortshöhe	WIEN (171)	Picturesque town · Elevation
Eine Reise wert	★★ MILANO	Worth a journey
Lohnt einen Umweg	★ TEMPLIN	Worth a detour
Sehenswert	Andermatt	Worth seeing

Landschaft / Landscape

Eine Reise wert	★★ Las Cañadas	Worth a journey
Lohnt einen Umweg	★ Texel	Worth a detour
Sehenswert	Dikti	Worth seeing

3 km

INDEX

This index lists all the main places, popular destinations and beaches, as well as some facts and persons mentioned in this guide. Numbers in bold indicate a main entry, italics a photograph.

Agullo, Ferran 8
Aiguablava 66
Aiguamolls de l'Empordà (National Park) 16, **59**, 90
Arenys de Mar 79
Artists' colony/Cadaqués 36
Banyoles 16, 19, 29
Barcelona 8, 9, 11, *12*, 13, 14, 15, 17, 19, 25, *26*, 27, 28, 29, **30**, 51, 84, 92, 98
Begur **65**, 92
Bellcaire d'Empordà *10*, 66
Besalú 29, *46*, **54**
Blanes 25, 28, *74*, **79**, 92
Cadaqués 5, 25, 29, *34*, **36**, 59, 90
Cala Llado/Roses 58
Cala Montgó/L'Escala 49
Cala Montjoi 90
Cala Mosca/Roses 58
Cala Murtra/Roses 58
Cala Petita/Portbou 45
Calella 21
Calella de Palafrugell *60*, **73**, 92
Calonge 28, **73**
Can Massaguer 16
Cantallops 45
Canyelles Grosses/Roses 58
Cap de Creus **40**, 90
Castell d'Aro 29, **82**
Castell Sant Salvador 44
Castelló d'Empúries **59**, 90
Colera 45
Cucurucuc de les Seves 40
Dalí, Salvador 8, **14**, 37, 39, *40*, 41, 52, **53**, 89
Dolmen de la Cova d'en Daina 73
Economy 19
El Cortalet 16, 59
El Far d'Empordà 55
El Pení **40**, 59
El Port de la Selva 25, **42**, 90
Empúriabrava 59
Empúries *15*, 47, **49**, *50*, 91

Ermita de Sant Elm 85
Ermita Santa Cristina **79**, *80*, 92
Es Pianc/Cadaqués 39
Es Poal/Cadaqués 39
Es Portal/Cadaqués 39
Figueres 14, 17, 28, **52**, 89, 97
Gaudí, Antoni 8, **15**, 30
Girona 8, 13, 25, 27, 28, 29, **68**, *70*, 91, 96, 97
Gulf of Roses 58
Illes Medes 16, **66**, 91
La Bisbal 25, **73**
La Garrotxa (volcanic landscape) 19
La Jonquera 45
La Molina 27
La Pera 91
L'Escala 19, 25, 29, **47**, 91, 97
L'Estartit 25, 28, 29, **61**, *64*, 91
L'Infern d'en Caixa 88
Llafranc **73**, 92
Llançà 25, 29, **41**, 90
Lloret de Mar 6, 10, 17, 21, 25, 28, 29, 75, **76**, 92
Mandíbula 16
Mas Rahola 59
Meda Gran 66
Medes Islands, see Illes Medes
Miró, Joan 8, **16**
Mont-Ras 94
Montroig 16
National Parks 16
Olot 19, 28, 29
Palafrugell 29, **73**, 92
Palamós 25, 28, 29, **71**, 92
Palau Saverdera 59
Pals 29, **67**, 92
Parc Natural dels Aiguamolls de l'Empordà 16, **59**, 90
Pedralta 85
Peralada 17, 55
Peratallada 67
Platja d'Aro 10, 25, 29, 75, **80**, *81*, 92
Platja d'Empúries/L'Escala 49

Platja de Fenals/Lloret de Mar 78
Platja de Pals **67**, 92
Platja de Riells/L'Escala 49
Platja de Sant Pol/Sant Feliu de Guíxols 85
Platja de Santa Margarita/Roses 58
Platja del Cau/Llançà 42
Port Lligat 6, 14, **40**, 90
Portbou 8, 28, **44**
Portdoguer/Cadaqués 39
Portitxó/Cadaqués 39
Púbol 91
Punta 92
Punta del Pi 42
Pyrenees 17
Ramblas 17
Ripoll 28
Romanya de la Selva 73
Roses 15, 19, 25, **56**, 90
S'Agaró 82
Sa Conca 40
San Miguel de Colera, see Colera
Sant Feliu de Guíxols 25, 28, 29, 75, **83**, 92
Sant Marti d'Empúries 51
Sant Miquel de Fluvià 51
Sant Pau 19
Sant Pere Pescador 28, **51**
Sant Pere de Rodes **43**, 59, 90
Santa Cristina d'Aro 28, **85**
Sardana 17
Separatism 18
Serra de Daró 91
Serra de Montseny 16
Sils 80
Tamariu **73**, 92
Tarragona 19
Torroella de Montgrí 25, 29, **61**, 91
Tossa de Mar 14, 25, 28, 75, **86**, 86, *87*, 92
Ullastret **67**, *68*, 91
Verges 27
Vilabertrán 56
Viladecanx 94
Water sports 39, 42, 45, 49, 58, 59, 65, 72, 78, 82, 85, 88

115

What do you get for your money?

Spain's reserve currency is the Peseta. Banknotes are in circulation in the following denominations, 1,000, 2,000, 5,000 and 10,000 ptas; coins are to the value of 1, 2, 5, 10, 25, 50, 100 and 500 ptas.

Prices on the Costa Brava fluctuate a great deal, depending on where you are: hotels, restaurants and bars in the tourist centres are bound to be more expensive than in, say, a tiny fishing village on the north coast. Prices given here are therefore average values. For example, a small cup of black coffee (café solo) costs between 120 and 150 ptas in a modest little bar. A small glass of beer, about the same. Coca-Cola approximately 180 ptas, a glass of wine 100–150 ptas, a hamburger, between 375 and 450 ptas, a cognac (medium quality), around 150 ptas, likewise a packet of cigarettes.

A taxi journey of around 5 km will set you back about 800 ptas. One litre of gas costs approximately 120 ptas, a small rent car costs approximately 8,000 ptas per day, including insurance. There are certain items that you should bring with you, since they are considerably more expensive in Spain,

such as batteries (for Walkmans, etc.), sun creme and film for your camera. A telephone call from Spain to another European country made on a mobile phone via the Spanish network costs between 100 and 200 ptas, depending on the provider.

Ptas	£	US$	Can$
100	0.36	0.51	0.76
250	0.91	1.28	1.90
500	1.82	2.56	3.80
750	2.72	3.84	5.69
1000	3.63	5.12	7.59
1500	5.45	7.68	11.39
2000	7.26	10.24	15.18
3000	10.89	15.35	22.77
4000	14.52	20.47	30.37
5000	18.15	25.59	37.96
6000	21.78	30.71	45.55
7500	27.23	38.39	56.94
10000	36.30	51.18	75.92
12500	45.38	63.98	94.90
15000	54.45	76.77	113.87
25000	90.75	127.95	189.79
40000	145.21	204.72	303.67
50000	181.51	255.90	379.58
75000	272.26	383.85	569.37
90000	326.71	460.62	683.25
100000	363.01	511.79	759.16